The Go-To Book for
Irish Crochet Motifs™

CONTENTS

INTRODUCTION   2

OVERVIEW   2

CHAPTER 1   4
STITCHES & TECHNIQUES
Covers padding cords and padded rings, bullion stitches, clones knots, picots, picot loops, cording, topstitching and joining.

CHAPTER 2   9
FLOWERS
Twenty-five flower motifs, such as the traditional Irish rose (several variations of the Irish rose are included), carnation, daisy and more. Traditional versions, plus updated versions are provided when possible.

CHAPTER 3   29
LEAVES
Chapter includes traditional versions, 14 different leaf styles, plus updated versions of the motifs when possible.

CHAPTER 4   39
FILL-IN MOTIFS
Twelve different motifs used to fill in spaces, including scrolls, wheels, fans, spokes, medallions, shamrocks and trefoils. Traditional versions are included, plus updated versions when possible.

CHAPTER 5   49
EDGINGS & INSERTIONS
This chapter contains 14 different types of edgings that can be used to edge Irish crochet pieces, towels and tablecloths. Traditional versions are included, plus updated versions when possible.

CHAPTER 6   58
DANGLES
Chapter contains eight different embellishments, such as the acorn, spirals and beads.

CHAPTER 7   63
OVERLAYS
This chapter includes four examples of how various motifs and shapes can be used together to give a total look to a flower, leaf or spray. Layering was a common method used in many vintage Irish crochet pieces.

CHAPTER 8   72
FILL-IN LACE
Six styles of fill-in lace are explained from basic chains, picot chains, clones knot chains and more.

CHAPTER 9   78
ASSEMBLY
This is the centerpiece for this book. It details how to put all the motifs into one piece and how to make fill-in lace to connect motifs.

Chapter includes: set up of motifs, discussion of various ways to accomplish a finished piece, sewing motifs on working cloth, working the fill-in lace, removing piece from working cloth and finishing.

CHAPTER 10   86
SQUARES & MOTIFS
Chapter includes five different motifs including traditional versions, plus updated versions when possible.

NOTE PAGES   92

STITCH GUIDE   94

METRIC CONVERSION CHARTS   95

Introduction

If you have ever tried to make an Irish crochet motif using vintage pattern books, you most likely ended up confused, frustrated and a bit bewildered.

The patterns are, at best, a bit vague. They are written in unclear versions and with imprecise wording that makes the patterns hard for the average crocheter to interpret. Some are almost impossible to decipher.

Therefore, a lot of these wonderful, beautiful motifs are unfortunately passed over.

My dream has been to take these lovely motifs and write them in such a manner that they make sense to the modern-day crocheter so that these stunning motifs will be preserved and used now and in the future.

Some motifs in this book are taken from antique patterns that are out of copyright, though all of the patterns in this book are rewritten and not copied, as written, from the antique patterns. That is the whole idea—to modernize the gorgeous motifs found in those old patterns.

However, some of the designs are original designs from me, the author.

—Kathryn White

Overview

With as many motifs as I thought were feasible, I have provided a traditional motif version with padding cords and padded rings, and then an updated version that doesn't use the padding cord and padded rings. For some motifs, though, the traditional version is the only way to provide the proper look of the motif. There are also some motifs that do not use padding cords or padded rings in the traditional versions.

If you see **Traditional** beside a motif name, it will incorporate padding cords and/or padded rings.

If you see **Updated** beside a motif name, it will not incorporate padding cords and/or padded rings.

If all you see is a name, then it will be appropriate as done for both traditional Irish crochet and updated Irish crochet.

If you see a **PC** and/or **PR** beside a motif name, it will require the use of padding cords (PC) or padded rings (PR) to make the motif.

SKILL LEVEL

Skill levels vary from easy to challenging depending on the motif and method used on the motif.

MATERIALS

I used size 10 crochet cotton in white for all motifs with one exception. For the 4th motif in overlays, I used a size 20 thread. Using a good quality thread/yarn will make crocheting easier and turn out a motif to be proud of.

All these motifs can be done in any desired-size thread or yarn. The size of your finished motif will vary according to the thread and hook sizes used.

I have used a size 7/1.65mm steel crochet hook for all but the motif done in size 20 thread. For that motif, I used a size 9/1.25mm steel crochet hook.

I used white throughout this book as it shows off the stitches well. I do encourage everyone to use the colors they prefer. Irish crochet is lovely when worked in classic white, in ecru or in eye-catching bright, vivid colors. The choice is always yours. I just want to provide you with the patterns for the motifs to make your Irish crochet dream a reality.

Dimensions: I have measured each motif across. I do not provide a gauge for each motif. Irish crochet is not an exact art form, so if your motifs vary slightly it will not matter.

Also, I encourage you to make these motifs in whatever size thread or yarn you are comfortable using. Gauge won't be relevant when changing the size of your thread or yarn and the hook size used to create your motifs.

TOOLS OF THE TRADE

Use a hook you are comfortable with for Irish crochet. Any type of hook works well as long as it is appropriate for the size of thread or yarn used. Remember that Irish crochet looks best if the stitches are firm. So you may want to use a smaller hook if your work is not as firm as you desire.

For the bullion stitch and the clones knot, you may want to use an inline hook as it makes it easier to draw through all the loops.

NONWORKING ENDS OF HOOKS OR RING MAKERS

Anything that you can wrap the thread or yarn around and slide it off easily will work for making your padding cord rings. In this book, I tell you to use the nonworking end of a crochet hook in a size that will give you the best size ring for the project when using size 10 thread. I do this simply because it works well, and most crocheters will have the hooks in their possession. I have used pencils, felt-tip markers, small dowels and wooden matches as needed to make rings. If you move up to a larger or smaller thread or yarn, you will need to adjust what you are using to create your rings.

SCISSORS

Good embroidery scissors are handy. These make it easier to cut your thread or yarn close to the work without snipping the actual piece.

STITCH MARKERS

Stitch markers can be used to mark stitches so you can easily find your place to work into later or to help keep count of stitches.

NEEDLES

You will have a lot of ends to sew in Irish crochet, so it is well worth investing in good tapestry needles that will fit your thread or yarn. A sharp tip works better than a blunt tip.

You may also need a regular sewing needle when assembling certain pieces, such as the overlay motifs.

I always try to use thread that matches my motif color when I do this.

FABRIC

If you decide to try doing a piece with fill-in lace, you will need some sort of fabric to sew your motifs to. This will keep your arrangement in place while you work the fill-in stitches. I have used brown paper bags and medium-weight fabric. You want a plain-color fabric so you can see your stitches. If your fabric is too lightweight, it won't keep your motif where you desire as you work; you don't want it so heavy that it is stiff to hold in your hand as you work.

PADDING CORD BOBBIN

The slotted plastic or cardboard cards designed to hold embroidery floss work well as a bobbin for your padding cord.

When you are asked to fold two longer lengths of padding cord to make a four-strand padding cord, attach cord to the bobbin starting at the cut end of the strands, and then wind around card until you have 8–10 inches of padding cord remaining. Slide strands in any slot to keep them from unwinding. Use the padding cord as needed. Unlock, unwind, and relock anytime the length of cord gets too short to be comfortable to work with. This allows you to use the longer lengths of padding cord without getting tangled or soiled.

STUFFING

You may need small amounts of fiberfill for some pieces, such as a ball or acorn. It will not take much. Yarn scraps of any color that will not show through the stitches will work also. ■

Chapter 1 STITCHES & TECHNIQUES

The Padded Ring is just what it sounds like—it's a series of sc crocheted over a wound-up piece of thread or yarn. This gives the ring a more 3-D look. This ring can attach to other pieces. Some will have picots and others will just be sc. Others may be the jumping-off point for a motif or design. But the basic technique is the same. The hardest part of making your ring is sliding the wound thread off whatever you wind it around and then sliding the crochet hook through the center without it falling apart. It does take practice, but it will get easier over time. The more winds you have on your wound thread, the more your ring is going to stand out. If this method eludes you and you still want the look of a padded ring, I do have a mock padding cord ring that can be used instead.

Padding cord ring (pc ring): This ring is made by wrapping your padding cord around the nonworking end of a crochet hook; size of hook varies according to size thread or yarn you are using and how big of a hole is desired in the middle. Normally 8–12 wraps is sufficient. The more wraps, the more dimensional it will be. Cut thread, leaving an inch or so of length, gently slide off and insert hook in ring, catch up your working thread and draw through, sc in ring. Follow instructions for the number of sc in ring.

Do not wrap too tightly or you will have trouble sliding it off the hook and retaining its shape. Leave about 1-inch length hanging at beg and end of wrap. This will make it easier to handle. Making these rings takes a little practice but gets easier as you go along.

PADDING CORD RINGS

BASIC RING

Example: Using nonworking end of size G hook and white, make a 12-wrap pc ring, 16 sc in ring, join in first sc of ring. Fasten off and weave in end.

This ring can be done with the nonworking end of any size hook to wrap your thread or yarn around to make the size ring desired or needed. The number of wraps can vary according to need or desire. The number of sts in the ring can vary according to desire or pattern requirements.

MOCK PADDING CORD RING

A padded ring using a simpler method than the traditional pc ring is worked in this manner:

Ch 5, join to form ring. Fasten off. Prepare another

ch-5 ring as previous ring, **do not fasten off**, ch 1, holding both rings tog, work required number of sts over both rings at the same time, work over the tails of the rings also. This will give you a padded ring. Work in ends of the tails and trim off excess. For an extra padded ring, make 3 rings instead of 2.

RING WITH PICOTS 6 POINTS

Using the nonworking end of size G hook and white, make a 12-wrap pc ring, 2 sc in ring, ch 3, (3 sc in ring, ch 3) 5 times, sc in ring, sl st in first sc. Fasten off, weave in end.

RING WITH PICOTS 8 POINTS

Using nonworking end of size G hook and white, make 12-wrap pc ring, sc in ring, ch 3, (2 sc in ring, ch 3) 7 times, sc in ring, sl st in first sc of rnd. Fasten off, weave in end.

CONNECTED RINGS

Ring 1 Using nonworking end of size G hook and white, make a 12-wrap pc ring, 12 sc in ring. Fasten off, weave in end.

Ring 2 Using nonworking end of size G hook and white, make a 12-wrap pc ring, 9 sc in ring, sl st in any sc on previous ring, 3 sc in ring. Fasten off, weave in end.

Rings 3–5 Using nonworking end of size G hook and white, make a 12-wrap pc ring, 9 sc in ring, sk 6 sc on previous ring from connection, sl st in next sc, 3 sc in ring. Fasten off, weave in end.

A padding cord is not all that difficult to do and adds so much to the motifs or designs. It gives so much more body to a piece that it is well worth the effort to learn the technique. This is important if you are doing a piece with fill-in lace, as the padding cord helps the piece hold its shape as worked and as it is used. Once you get used to carrying 4–6 strands of thread along with your work and learn to keep the tension even, it really isn't that hard to use. For most motifs and pieces in this book, I chose to use 4 strands of thread. This is a doable number for learning the technique.

You will need to learn to be aware of your padding cord. Making sure all strands are flat under the sts. Adjust tension often on rows or rnds. It is a good idea to check it before making a turn like at the top of a petal. Do not tighten your tension of padding cord too much as this can make your piece buckle. If the padding cord tension is too loose the padding cord may stick out of your sts.

You can vary the size of the padding cord by the size of thread used and/or by the number of strands carried along. It is easier to use less strands of a larger size thread or yarn than to use lots of strands of a smaller size thread or yarn. If using a colored thread, use 4–6 strands of the same thread so that it matches. One of the nice things about using a padding cord on a piece or motif is that you can adjust it a bit just by moving the sc over the padding cord, either tighter or looser as needed, to get the shape or look you want.

The amounts I have given in this book are not exact. I have tried to be generous in the amounts. This is better than not enough. Use the leftover ends to make pc rings.

Remember, the size thread or yarn you are using will change the length needed for your padding cord in the motifs in this book. If you are using size 30 thread, you will need less length. If you choose to use a larger thread or yarn, you will need a longer length.

Weave the ends in the same manner as working in any other end.

PADDING CORD SAMPLES

Cut 2 lengths of thread for padding cord as indicated in instructions, hold tog and fold in half, wrap on padding cord bobbin.

Work st in indicated st and through the fold of padding cord threads, working over all 4 strands of padding cord and in the sts as indicated in pattern.

PADDING CORD WORKED IN CHAIN

PADDING CORD WORKED IN SC FOUNDATION

PADDING CORD WORKED IN CH FOUNDATION WITH 2ND ROW OF PADDING CORD

PADDING CORD BASE

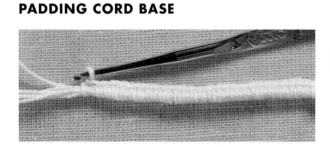

EXAMPLE

Cut 2 lengths of thread for padding cord as indicated in instructions. Hold tog and fold in half, wrap on padding cord bobbin. Draw up a thread through the fold of padding cord, ch 1, sc, working over all 4 strands of padding cord, continue making sc over the strands of padding cord as required for length or as pattern indicates.

MOTIF STARTED OVER PADDING CORD INSTEAD OF ON A RING

Some motifs can be started over the padding cord alone, such as this flower.

STEM WITH PICOTS

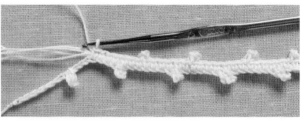

PADDING CORD LENGTHS

Cut 2 lengths of thread for padding cord, double the length needed for stem desired plus a couple of inches more, hold tog and fold in half, wrap on padding cord bobbin.

[Ch 10, sl st in 4th ch from hook] as many times as desired, ch 6, sc in 2nd ch from hook and through the fold of the padding cord, working over all 4 strands of padding cord across, sc in next ch st, ch 3 picot in last sc made, (sc in next 6 ch sts, ch 3 picot in last sc made) rep as needed, ending with sc in rem ch sts.

Ch-3 Picot: Ch 3, sl st in top of indicated st.

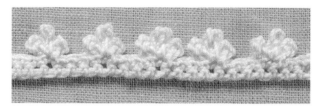

TRIPLE PICOT

Ch 4, sl st in front lp at the top of the last st made and in front strand of the same st, ch 4, sl st in the same st again, catching the front lp of sl st from ch-4 lp, ch 4, sl st in the same st again, catching front lp of sl sts from first and 2nd ch-4 lps.

BULLION STITCH

Wrap thread around hook the number of times indicated in pattern. Insert hook in indicated st, draw lp through, yo and draw through all lps on hook, do not draw up tight, yo and draw through lp to lock st.

This is a st that is a little difficult the first few times.

HINTS

Use an inline hook. An inline hook will be the same width from the head of the hook down through the throat of the hook. If it tapers down to the neck it is going to be more difficult to work with and will not work nearly as well.

When you have drawn the thread through the indicated st, let the thread relax for a second before completing the st.

Keep your tension fairly loose. Relax your thread hand a little before drawing through the lps (*9 wraps were used in the sample*). When starting to learn this st, work with fewer lps on the hook—4 or 5 are a good starting point.

CLONES KNOT

This st is worked over ch sts in the following manner: ch 8 (yo, draw up a lp reaching under the front of the ch st, yo, draw up a lp reaching under the back of the ch) rep twice more, yo draw up lp reaching under the front of the ch, yo, draw through all 18 lps on hook, sl st in 5th ch st, draw up gently until the beg and end of clones knot almost meet, sc around the ch, continue ch sts as desired.

This is like the bullion st and it works best with an inline hook. You can vary the number of chs between the clones knots and you can vary the number of times you catch up the lps.

POPCORN STITCH

Do the required number of dc in 1 st or sp as indicated, remove hook from lp, insert hook in top of first st of group, pick up dropped lp and draw through. To have the popcorn face the front of the work, insert hook from front to back. To have the popcorn face the back side of the work, insert the hook from back to front.

ROMANIAN POINT LACE CORD

Ch 2, sc in 2nd ch from hook, rotate piece away from you (*always rotate in the same direction*) sc in the single lp of last ch made, rotate piece away from you until you are looking at the back side of piece, you will now see 2 lps at the base of the last sc you made, these will be to the side and toward the top, work 1 sc in these 2 lps, *rotate cord away from you, sc in the 2 lps at base of previous sc, rep from * until cord measures length desired.

CORD #1 WORKED IN BACK LPS

Ch 5, join to form a ring.

Rnd 1 (RS): 8 sc in ring, join in back lp of first sc.

Rnd 2: Ch 1, working in back lp only, sc in each sc around, join in back lp of first sc.

Rep rnd 2 until cord measures length desired. Fasten off. Weave in ends.

CORD #2

Ch 5, sl st to form ring, ch 1, 8 sc in ring, sc in each sc around, do not join but keep working around in a spiral, sc in each st until length desired. Fasten off. Weave in ends.

SPECIAL STITCHES

Extended double crochet (edc): Done in this manner: beg normal dc until 3 lps rem on hook, yo, draw through 1 lp *(3 lps on hook)*, [yo, draw through 2 lps on hook] twice. This creates a slightly taller than normal dc.

Extended treble crochet (etr): Done in this manner: beg normal tr until 4 lps rem on hook, yo, draw through 1 lp *(4 lps on hook)*, [yo, draw through 2 lps on hook] 3 times. This creates a slightly taller than normal tr.

Extended double treble (edtr): Done in this manner: beg normal dtr until 5 lps rem on hook, yo, draw through 1 lp *(5 lps on hook)*, [yo, draw through 2 lps on hook] 4 times. This creates a slightly taller than normal dtr.

Double treble joining (dtr joining): Holding last lp of each st on hook [dtr in indicated st or sp] twice, yo, draw through all lps on hook.

3-double crochet cluster (3-dc cl): Holding the last lp of each st on hook, 3 dc in indicated st or sp, yo, draw through all lps on hook.

3-treble crochet cluster (3-tr cl): Holding last lp of each st on hook, 3 tr in indicated st or sp, yo, draw through all lps on hook.

3-double treble cluster (3-dtr cl): Holding last lp of each st on hook, 3 dtr in indicated st, yo, draw through all lps on hook.

Single crochet decrease (sc dec): Insert hook in indicated st or sp and draw up a lp, insert hook in next st or sp, yo, draw up a lp *(3 lps on hook)*, yo, draw through all lps on hook.

Double crochet decrease (dc dec): Start a dc in first st, yo, draw through 2 lps on hook, beg another dc in next st, yo, draw through 2 lps, yo, draw through rem lps.

Join: Join each round with sl st as indicated unless otherwise stated.

Quadruple treble (quad tr): Yo hook 5 times, insert hook in indicated st, yo, draw up a lp, [yo, draw through 2 lps on hook] 6 times. ■

Chapter 2 FLOWERS

Almost always, the first thing that attracts us to Irish crochet is beautiful flowers that can be created with this method of crocheting. There are so many wonderful flower designs out there, I was hard-pressed to choose which ones to concentrate on. I decided to concentrate on flowers that are fairly easily done or easily translated to an updated version.

Whether you decide to make your pieces in the traditional manner with padded rings and padding cords or as an updated version, you should be able to find enough to create your own beautiful Irish crochet pieces or use them as accents on a hat, jewelry, pillow, scarf, sweater or whatever you choose.

1. SMALL FILL-IN FLOWER 1

SKILL LEVEL

EASY

FINISHED MEASUREMENT
¾ inch across

MATERIALS
- Size 10 crochet cotton: 5 yds white
- Size 7/1.65mm steel crochet hook

Rnd 1: Ch 4, join to form a ring, (ch 2, 3 dc in ring, ch 2, sl st in ring) 5 times. Fasten off. Weave in end.

2. SMALL FILL-IN FLOWER 2

SKILL LEVEL

EASY

FINISHED MEASUREMENT
1 inch across

MATERIALS
- Size 10 crochet cotton: 5 yds white
- Size 7/1.65mm steel crochet hook

Rnd 1: Ch 4, join to form a ring, ch 1, 12 sc in ring, join in front lp of first sc.

Rnd 2: Ch 1, working in front lp only, (sc, ch3) twice in same sc, rep from * around, join in first sc. Fasten off. Weave in ends.

3. STAR FLOWER

SKILL LEVEL
INTERMEDIATE

FINISHED MEASUREMENT
1¼ inches across

MATERIALS
- Size 10 crochet cotton: 7 yds white
- Size 7/1.65mm steel crochet hook

Rnd 1: Ch 4 (*counts as first tr*), holding last lp of st on hook, 2 tr in 4th ch from hook (*the 4th ch is the ch you will work all your petals in*), yo and draw through all lps on hook, ch 3, sl st in top of cluster just made (*ch-3 picot made*), ch 4, sl st in base of tr cl, (ch 3, holding last lp of st on the hook, 2 tr in same ch as last petal, yo and draw through all lps on hook, ch-3 picot in top of cl just made, ch 4, sl st in same ch as last petal) 4 times (*5 petals*). Fasten off. Weave in ends.

4A. SMALL 6-PETAL FLOWER WITH PICOTS: TRADITIONAL WITH PC & PR

SKILL LEVEL
◼◼◼▢
INTERMEDIATE

FINISHED MEASUREMENT
1½ inches across

MATERIALS

- Size 10 crochet cotton:
  15 yds white
- Size 7/1.65mm steel crochet hook
- Size I/9/5.5mm crochet hook for pc

Padding cord lengths: Cut 2 lengths of white thread 15 inches long for padding cord, hold tog and fold in half.

With white, start a pc ring of 12 wraps over nonworking end of size I hook.

Rnd 1: 3 sc in ring, ch-3 picot in last sc made, (4 sc in ring, ch-3 picot in last sc made) 5 times, ending with sc in ring, join in first sc.

Rnd 2: Ch 1, sc in same sc and through the fold of the padding cord threads, working over all 4 strands of padding cord, [(4 sc over padding cord alone, ch-3 picot in last sc made) twice, 3 sc over padding cord alone, sk next 3 sc, sc in next sc] 6 times, ending with sl st in first sc. Fasten off. Weave in end and padding cords ends.

4B. SMALL 6-PETAL FLOWER WITH PICOTS: UPDATED VERSION

SKILL LEVEL
◼◼◼▢
INTERMEDIATE

FINISHED MEASUREMENT
1½ inches across

MATERIALS
- Size 10 crochet cotton:
  15 yds white
- Size 7/1.65mm steel crochet hook

Rnd 1: Ch 7, join to form a ring, ch 1, 3 sc in ring, ch-3 picot in last sc made, (4 sc in ring, ch-3 picot in last sc made) 5 times, ending with a sc in ring, join in first sc.

Rnd 2: Ch 1, sc in same sc, ch 7, sk next 3 sc, *sc in next sc, ch 7, sk next 3 sc, rep from * around, join in first sc.

Rnd 3: Ch 1, sc in same sc, (4 sc in ch-7 sp, ch-3 picot in last sc made) twice, 3 sc in same sp, *sc in next sc, (4 sc in ch-7 sp, ch-3 picot in last sc made) twice, 3 sc in same sp, rep from * around, join in first sc. Fasten off. Weave in ends.

ROSES
BASIC IRISH CROCHET ROSES

There are many ways to make the traditional Irish crochet roses. I am going to cover a lot of them, but there are more possibilities. This will give you a good grounding in the Irish roses and some of their variations.

5. A, B & C 6-PETAL ROSE 1, 2 & 3 LAYERS: TRADITIONAL & UPDATED

SKILL LEVEL

INTERMEDIATE

FINISHED MEASUREMENTS

1⅛ inches across, 1⅜ inches across and 1½ inches across

MATERIALS
- Size 10 crochet cotton: 10, 20 or 30 yds white
- Size 7/1.65mm steel crochet hook
- Size G/6/4mm crochet hook for pc

Rnd 1: Using the nonworking end of a size G hook, with white, make a 12-wrap pc ring, 12 sc in ring, join in first sc (*traditional*); or ch 5, join to form ring (*updated*), 12 sc in ring, join in first sc.

Rnd 2: Ch 1, sc in same sc, ch 3, sk next sc, *sc in next sc, ch 3, sk next sc, rep from * around, join in first sc. (*6 ch 3 lps*)

Rnd 3: Sl st in ch-3 lp, ch 1, *(sc, 5 dc, sc) in same ch-3 lp, rep from * in each ch-3 lp around, join in first sc. (*6 petals*)

Note: *At this point, a 1-layer rose is completed. You can end off at this point or continue for more layers.*

Rnd 4: Ch 1, working behind petals just completed, work sc around first sc of rnd 2, ch 4, *sc around next sc on rnd 2, ch 4, rep from * around, join in first sc. (*6 ch-4 lps*)

Rnd 5: Sl st in ch-4 lp, ch 1, *(sc, 7 dc, sc) in the same ch-4 lp, rep from * in each ch-4 lp around, join in first sc. (*6 petals*)

Note: *At this point a 2-layer rose is completed. You can end off at this point or continue for more layers.*

Rnd 6: Ch 1, working behind petals just completed, work sc around first sc of rnd 4, ch 5, *sc around next sc on rnd 4, ch 5, rep from * around, join in first sc. (*6 ch 5-lps*)

Rnd 7: Sl st in ch-5 lp, ch 1, *(sc, 9 dc, sc) in the same ch-5 lp, rep from * in each ch-5 lp around, join in first sc. Fasten off. Weave in ends. (*6 petals*)

Note: *You can create more layers of petals on your roses by following this formula: Add 1 ch to each ch-lp on the set-up rnd behind the previous petal. Add 2 dc to each petal on the next rnd.*

6. A, B & C 8-PETAL ROSE 1, 2 & 3 LAYERS: TRADITIONAL & UPDATED

SKILL LEVEL

INTERMEDIATE

FINISHED MEASUREMENTS

1⅜ inches across, 1½ inches across and 1⅝ inches across

MATERIALS
- Size 10 crochet cotton:
  10, 20 or 30 yds white
- Size 7/1.65mm steel crochet hook
- Size G/6/4mm crochet hook for pc

Rnd 1: Using nonworking end of size G hook, with white, make a 12-wrap pc ring, 16 sc in ring, sl st in first sc in ring *(traditional)*; or ch 5, join to form ring *(updated)*, 16 sc in ring, join in first sc.

Rnd 2: Ch 1, sc in same sc, ch 3, sk next sc, *sc in next sc, ch 3, sk next sc, rep from * around, join in first sc. *(8 ch-3 lps)*

Rnd 3: Sl st in ch-3 lp, ch 1, *(sc, 5 dc, sc) in same ch-3 lp, rep from * in each ch-3 lp around, join in first sc. *(8 petals)*

Note: *At this point, a 1-layer rose is completed. You can end off at this point or continue for more layers.*

Rnd 4: Ch 1, working behind the petals just finished, work a sc around first sc from rnd 2, ch 4, *sc around next sc on rnd 2, ch 4, rep from * around, join in first sc. *(8 ch-4 lps)*

Rnd 5: Sl st in ch-4 lp, ch 1, *(sc, 7 dc, sc) in same ch-4 lp, rep from * in each ch-4 lp around, join in first sc. *(8 petals)*

Note: *At this point, a 2-layer rose is completed. You can end off at this point or continue for more layers.*

Rnd 6: Ch 1, working behind the petals just finished, work a sc around first sc on rnd 4, ch 5, *sc around next sc on rnd 4, ch 5, rep from * around, join in first sc. *(8 ch-5 lps)*

Rnd 7: Sl st in ch-5 lp, ch 1, *(sc, 9 dc, sc) in same ch-5 lp, rep from * in each ch-5 lp around, join in first sc. Fasten off. Weave in ends. *(8 petals)*

Note: *You can create more layers of petals on your roses by following this formula: Add 1 ch to each ch-lp on the set-up rnd behind the previous petal. Add 2 dc to each petal on the next rnd.*

7. A, B & C 6-PETAL ROSE WITH PICOTS 1, 2 & 3 LAYERS: TRADITIONAL & UPDATED

SKILL LEVEL

INTERMEDIATE

FINISHED MEASUREMENTS
1½ inches across, 1⅝ inches across and 2 inches across

MATERIALS
- Size 10 crochet cotton:
  10, 20 or 30 yds white
- Size 7/1.65mm steel crochet hook
- Size G/6/4mm crochet hook for pc

Rnd 1: Using nonworking end of size G hook, with white, make a 12-wrap pc ring, 12 sc in ring, sl st in first sc *(traditional)*; or ch 5, join to form ring, *(updated)* 12 sc in ring, join in first sc.

Rnd 2: Ch 1, sc in same sc, ch 3, sk next sc, *sc in next sc, ch 3, sk next sc, rep from * around, join in first sc. *(6 ch 3-lps)*

Rnd 3: Sl st in ch-3 lp, ch 1, *(sc, 3 dc, ch-3 picot in last dc made, 2 dc, sc) in same ch-3 lp, rep from * in each ch-3 lp around, join in first sc. *(6 petals)*

Note: *At this point, a 1-layer rose is completed. You can end off at this point or continue for more layers.*

Rnd 4: Ch 1, working behind the petals just finished, work a sc around first sc from rnd 2, ch 4, *sc around next sc on rnd 2, ch 4, rep from * around, join in first sc. *(6 ch-4 lps)*

Rnd 5: Sl st in ch-4 lp, ch 1, *(sc, 4 dc, ch-3 picot in last dc made, 3 dc, sc) in same ch-4 lp, rep from * in each ch-4 lp around, join in first sc. *(6 petals)*

Note: *At this point, a 2-layer rose is completed. You can end off at this point or continue for more layers.*

Rnd 6: Ch 1, working behind the petals just finished, work a sc around first sc on rnd 4, ch 5, *sc around next sc on rnd 4, ch 5, rep from * around, join in first sc. *(6 ch-5 lps)*

Rnd 7: Sl st in ch-5 lp, ch 1, *(sc, 4 dc, ch-3 picot in last dc made, 3 dc, sc) in same ch-5 lp, rep from * in each ch-5 lp around, join in first sc. Fasten off. Weave in ends. *(6 petals)*

8. A, B & C 8-PETAL ROSE WITH PICOTS 1, 2 & 3 LAYERS: TRADITIONAL & UPDATED

SKILL LEVEL

INTERMEDIATE

FINISHED MEASUREMENTS
1½ inches across, 1¾ inches across and 2⅛ inches across

MATERIALS
- Size 10 crochet cotton:
  15, 25 or 35 yds white
- Size 7/1.65mm steel crochet hook
- Size G/6/4mm crochet hook for pc

Rnd 1: Using the nonworking end of a size G hook, with white, make a 12-wrap pc ring, 16 sc in ring, sl st in first sc *(traditional)*; or ch 5, join to form ring *(updated)*, 16 sc in ring, join in first sc.

Rnd 2: Ch 1, sc in same sc, ch 3, sk next sc, *sc in next sc, ch 3, sk next sc, rep from * around, join in first sc. *(8 ch-3 lps)*

Rnd 3: Sl st in ch-3 lp, ch 1, *(sc, 3 dc, ch-3 picot in last dc made, 2 dc, sc) in same ch-3 lp, rep from * in each lp around, join in first sc. *(8 petals)*

Note: *At this point, a 1-layer rose is completed. You can end off at this point or continue for more layers.*

Rnd 4: Ch 1, working behind the petals just finished, work sc around first sc from rnd 2, ch 4, *sc around next sc on rnd 2, ch 4, rep from * around, join in first sc. *(8 ch-4 lps)*

Rnd 5: Sl st in ch-4 lp, ch 1, *(sc, 4 dc, ch-3 picot in last dc made, 3 dc, sc) in same ch-4 lp, rep from * in each lp around, join in first sc. *(8 petals)*

Note: *At this point, a 2-layer rose is completed. You can end off at this point or continue for more layers.*

Rnd 6: Ch 1, working behind the petals just finished, work sc around first sc on rnd 4, ch 5, *sc around next sc on rnd 4, ch 5, rep from * around, join in first sc. *(8 ch-5 lps)*

Rnd 7: Sl st in ch-5 lp, ch 1, *(sc, 4 dc, ch-3 picot in last dc made, 3 dc, sc) in same ch-5 lp, rep from * in each lp around, join in first sc. Fasten off. Weave in ends. *(8 petals)*

9. A, B & C 6-PETAL FRILLED ROSE 1, 2 & 3 LAYERS: TRADITIONAL & UPDATED

SKILL LEVEL

INTERMEDIATE

FINISHED MEASUREMENTS

1½ inches across, 1⅝ inches across and 1⅞ inches across

MATERIALS

- Size 10 crochet cotton:
  10, 20 or 30 yds white
- Size 7/1.65mm steel crochet hook
- Size G/6/4mm crochet hook for pc

Rnd 1: Using the nonworking end of a size G hook, with white, make a 12-wrap pc ring, 12 sc in ring, sl st in first sc (*traditional*); or ch 5, join to form ring (*updated*), 12 sc in ring, join in first sc.

Rnd 2: Ch 1, sc in same sc, ch 3, sk next sc, *sc in next sc, ch 3, sk next sc, rep from * around, join in first sc. (*6 ch-3 lps*)

Rnd 3: Sl st in ch-3 lp, ch 1, *(sc, 5 dc, sc) in same ch-3 lp, rep from * in each lp around, join in first sc. (*6 petals*)

Rnd 4: Ch 1, sc in same st, (ch 2, sc in next dc) 5 times, ch 2, sc in next sc, *sc in next sc, (ch 2, sc in next dc) 5 times, ch 2, sc in next sc, rep from * around, join in first sc.

Note: *At this point, a 1-layer rose is completed. You can end off at this point or continue for more layers.*

Rnd 5: Ch 2, working behind the petals just finished, work sc around first sc from rnd 2, ch 4, *sc around next sc on rnd 2, ch 4, rep from * around, join in first sc. (*6 ch-4 lps*)

Rnd 6: Sl st in ch-4 lp, ch 1, *(sc, 7 dc, sc) in same ch-4 lp, rep from * in each ch-4 lp around, join in first sc. (*6 petals*)

Rnd 7: Ch 1, sc in same st, (ch 2, sc in next dc) 7 times, ch 2, sc in next sc, *sc in next sc, (ch 2, sc in next dc) 7 times, ch 2, sc in next sc, rep from * around, join in first sc.

Note: *At this point, a 2-layer rose is completed. You can end off at this point or continue for more layers.*

Rnd 8: Ch 2, working behind the petals just finished, work sc around first sc from rnd 5, ch 5, *sc around next sc on rnd 5, ch 5, rep from * around, join in first sc. (*6 ch-5 lps*)

Rnd 9: Sl st in ch-5 lp, ch 1, *(sc, 9 dc, sc) in same ch-5 lp, rep from * in each ch-5 lp around, join in first sc. (*6 petals*)

Rnd 10: Ch 1, sc in same st, (ch 2, sc in next dc) 9 times, ch 2, sc in next sc, *sc in next sc, (ch 2, sc in next dc) 9 times, ch 2, sc in next sc, rep from * around, join in first sc. Fasten off. Weave in ends.

Note: *You can create more layers of petals on your roses by following this formula: Add 1 ch to each ch-lp on the set-up rnd behind the previous petal. Add 2 dc to each petal on the next rnd. Add 2 (ch 2, sc) to each petal.*

10. A, B & C 8-PETAL FRILLED ROSE 1, 2 & 3 LAYERS: TRADITIONAL & UPDATED

SKILL LEVEL

INTERMEDIATE

FINISHED MEASUREMENTS

1⅝ inches across, 1¾ inches across and 2 inches across

MATERIALS

- Size 10 crochet cotton:
  15, 25 or 35 yds white
- Size 7/1.65mm steel crochet hook
- Size G/6/4mm crochet hook for pc

Rnd 1: Using the nonworking end of a size G hook, with white, make a 12-wrap pc ring, 16 sc in ring, sl st in first sc (*traditional*); or ch 5, join to form ring (*updated*), 16 sc in ring, join in first sc.

Rnd 2: Ch 1, sc in same sc, ch 3, sk next sc, *sc in next sc, ch 3, sk next sc, rep from * around, join in first sc. (*8 ch-3 lps*)

Rnd 3: Sl st in ch-3 lp, ch 1, *(sc, 5 dc, sc) in same ch-3 lp, rep from * in each lp around, join in first sc. (*8 petals*)

Rnd 4: Ch 1, sc in same st, (ch 2, sc in next dc) 5 times, ch 2, sc in next sc, *sc in next sc, (ch 2, sc in next dc) 5 times, ch 2, sc in next sc, rep from * around, join in first sc.

Note: *At this point, a 1-layer rose is completed. You can end off at this point or continue for more layers.*

Rnd 5: Ch 2, working behind the petals just finished, work sc around first sc from rnd 2, ch 4, *sc around next sc on rnd 2, ch 4, rep from * around, join in first sc. (*8 ch-4 lps*)

Rnd 6: Sl st in ch-4 lp, ch 1, *(sc, 7 dc, sc) in same ch-4 lp, rep from * in each ch-4 lp around, join in first sc. (*8 petals*)

Rnd 7: Ch 1, sc in same st, (ch 2, sc in next dc) 7 times, ch 2, sc in next sc, *sc in next sc, (ch 2, sc in next dc) 7 times, ch 2, sc in next sc, rep from * around, join in first sc.

Note: *At this point, a 2-layer rose is completed. You can end off at this point or continue for more layers.*

Rnd 8: Ch 2, working behind the petals just finished, work sc around first sc from rnd 5, ch 5, *sc around next sc on rnd 5, ch 5, rep from * around, join in first sc. (*8 ch-5 lps*)

Rnd 9: Sl st in ch-5 lp, ch 1, *(sc, 9 dc, sc) in same ch-5 lp, rep from * in each ch-5 lp around, join in first sc. (*8 petals*)

Rnd 10: Ch 1, sc in same st, (ch 2, sc in next dc) 9 times, ch 2, sc in next sc, *sc in next sc, (ch 2, sc in next dc) 9 times, ch 2, sc in next sc, rep from * around, join in first sc. Fasten off. Weave in ends.

Note: *You can create more layers of petals on your roses by following this formula: Add 1 ch to each ch-lp on the set-up rnd behind the previous petal. Add 2 dc to each petal on the next rnd. Add 2 (ch 2, sc) to each petal.*

11. 6-PETAL ROSE OFFSET PETALS: TRADITIONAL & UPDATED

SKILL LEVEL

INTERMEDIATE

FINISHED MEASUREMENT

1¾ inches across

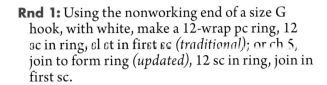

MATERIALS

- Size 10 crochet cotton:
  25 yds white
- Size 7/1.65mm steel crochet hook
- Size G/6/4mm crochet hook for pc

Rnd 1: Using the nonworking end of a size G hook, with white, make a 12-wrap pc ring, 12 sc in ring, sl st in first sc *(traditional)*; or ch 5, join to form ring *(updated)*, 12 sc in ring, join in first sc.

Rnd 2: Ch 1, sc in same sc, ch 3, sk next sc, *sc in next sc, ch 3, sk next sc, rep from * around, join in first sc. *(6 ch-3 lps)*

Rnd 3: Sl st in ch-3 lp, ch 1, *(sc, 6 dc, sc) in same ch-3 lp, rep from * in each lp around, join in first sc. *(6 petals)*

Rnd 4: Sl st across back of sc and 3 dc at base of sts, sl st over ch-3 lp of rnd 2 between 3rd and 4th dc of rnd 3, ch 1, sc in same lp, ch 4, *sc over ch-3 lp of rnd 2 between the 3rd and 4th dc on next petal, ch 4, rep from * around, join in first sc. *(6 ch-4 lps)*

Rnd 5: Sl st in ch-4 lp, ch 1, *(sc, 8 dc, sc) in same ch-4 lp, rep from * in each ch-4 lp around, join in first sc. *(6 petals)*

Rnd 6: Sl st across back of sc and 4 dc at base of sts, sl st over ch-4 lp of rnd 4 between 4th and 5th dc of rnd 5, ch 1, sc in same lp, ch 5, *sc over ch-4 lp of rnd 4 between 4th and 5th dc on next petal, ch 5, rep from * around, join in first sc. *(6 ch-5 lps)*

Rnd 7: Sl st in ch-5 lp, ch 1, *(sc, 10 dc, sc) in same ch-5 lp, rep from * in each ch-5 lp around, join in first sc. Fasten off. Weave in ends. *(6 petals)*

12. 8-PETAL ROSE OFFSET PETALS: TRADITIONAL & UPDATED

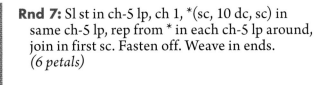

SKILL LEVEL

INTERMEDIATE

FINISHED MEASUREMENT

2⅛ inches across

MATERIALS

- Size 10 crochet cotton:
  30 yds white
- Size 7/1.65mm steel crochet hook
- Size G/6/4mm crochet hook for pc

Rnd 1: Using the nonworking end of a size G hook, with white, make a 12-wrap pc ring, 16 sc in ring, sl st in first sc *(traditional)*; or ch 5, sl st to form ring *(updated)*, 16 sc in ring, join in first sc.

Rnd 2: Ch 1, sc in same sc, ch 3, sk next sc, *sc in next sc, ch 3, sk next sc, rep from * around, join in first sc. *(8 ch-3 lps)*

Rnd 3: Sl st in ch-3 lp, ch 1, *(sc, 6 dc, sc) in same ch-3 lp, rep from * in each lp around, join in first sc. *(8 petals)*

Rnd 4: Sl st across back of sc and 3 dc at base of sts, sl st over ch-3 lp of rnd 2 between 3rd and 4th dc of rnd 3, ch 1, sc in same lp, ch 4, *sc over ch-3 lp of rnd 2 between the 3rd and 4th dc on next petal, ch 4, rep from * around, join in first sc. *(8 ch-4 lps)*

Rnd 5: Sl st in ch-4 lp, ch 1, *(sc, 8 dc, sc) in same ch-4 lp, rep from * in each ch-4 lp around, join in first sc. *(8 petals)*

Rnd 6: Sl st across back of sc and 4 dc at base of sts, sl st over ch-4 lp of rnd 4 between 4th and 5th dc of rnd 5, ch 1, sc in same lp, ch 5, *sc over ch-4 lp of rnd 4 between 4th and 5th dc on next petal, ch 5, rep from * around, join in first sc. *(8 ch-5 lps)*

Rnd 7: Sl st in ch-5 lp, ch 1, *(sc, 10 dc, sc) in same ch-5 lp, rep from * in each ch-5 lp around, join in first sc. Fasten off. Weave in ends. *(8 petals)*

13A. 6-PETAL DAISY: TRADITIONAL WITH PC AND PR

SKILL LEVEL

INTERMEDIATE

FINISHED MEASUREMENT
2 inches across

MATERIALS
- Size 10 crochet cotton:
  20 yds white
- Size 7/1.65mm steel crochet hook
- Size G/6/4mm crochet hook for pc

Padding cord lengths: With white, cut 2 lengths of thread 1 yd long for padding cord, hold tog and fold in half, wrap on padding cord bobbin.

Rnd 1: Using nonworking end of a size G hook, with white, make a 12-wrap pc ring, 12 sc in ring, join in first sc.

Rnd 2: Working in back lp only, ch 1, sc in same sc, ch 8, sc in 2nd ch from hook, hdc in next ch st, dc in each of next 3 ch sts, hdc in next ch st, sc in next ch st, sl st in next sc, *sc in next sc, ch 8, sc in 2nd ch from hook, hdc in next ch st, dc in each of next 3 ch sts, hdc in next ch st, sc in next ch st, sl st in next sc, rep from * around, join in first sc.

Rnd 3: Ch 1, sc in both lps of first sc on rnd 1, and through the fold of the padding cord threads, work over all 4 strands of the padding

cord threads around, working up the back side of ch, sc in each of next ch 7 sts, 3 sc in tip of petal, sc in next sc, sc in next hdc, sc in each of next 3 dc, sc in next hdc, sc in next sc, *sc in both lps of sc on rnd 1, working up the back side of ch, sc in each of next ch 7 sts, 3 sc in tip of petal, sc in next sc, sc in next hdc, sc in each of next 3 dc, sc in next hdc, sc in next sc, rep from * around, join in first sc. Fasten off. Weave in ends.

13B. 6-PETAL DAISY: UPDATED

SKILL LEVEL

INTERMEDIATE

FINISHED MEASUREMENT
2¼ inches across

MATERIALS
- Size 10 crochet cotton:
  20 yds white
- Size 7/1.65mm steel crochet hook

Rnd 1: Ch 5, join to form ring, 12 sc in ring, join in back lp of first sc in ring.

Rnd 2: Working in back lp only, ch 1, sc in same sc, ch 8, sc in 2nd ch from hook, hdc in next ch st, dc in each of next 3 ch sts, hdc in next ch st, sc in next ch st, sl st in next sc, *sc in next sc, ch 8, sc in 2nd ch from hook, hdc in next ch st, dc in each of next 3 ch sts, hdc in next ch st, sc in next ch st, sl st in next sc, rep from * around, join in first sc.

Rnd 3: Ch 1, sc in both lps of first sc on rnd 1, working up the back side of ch, sc in each of next ch 7 sts, 3 sc in tip of petal, sc in next sc, sc in next hdc, sc in each of next 3 dc, sc in next hdc, sc in next sc, *sc in both lps of sc on rnd 1, working up the back side of ch, sc in each of next ch 7 sts, 3 sc in tip of petal, sc in next sc, sc in next hdc, sc in each of next 3 dc, sc in next hdc, sc in next sc, rep from * around, join in first sc. Fasten off. Weave in ends.

14. SIMPLE 12-PETAL DAISY SMALL: TRADITIONAL & UPDATED

SKILL LEVEL

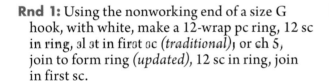

INTERMEDIATE

FINISHED MEASUREMENT
1¾ inches across

MATERIALS
- Size 10 crochet cotton:
    10 yds white
- Size 7/1.65mm steel crochet hook
- Size G/6/4mm crochet hook for pc

Rnd 1: Using the nonworking end of a size G hook, with white, make a 12-wrap pc ring, 12 sc in ring, sl st in first sc (*traditional*); or ch 5, join to form ring (*updated*), 12 sc in ring, join in first sc.

Rnd 2: Ch 1, sc in same sc, ch 7, sc in 2nd ch from hook, hdc in next ch st, dc in each of next 2 ch sts, hdc in next ch st, sc in next ch st, sl st in same sc in ring, *sc in next sc, ch 7, sc in 2nd ch from hook, hdc in next ch st, dc in each of next 2 ch sts, hdc in next ch st, sc in next ch st, sl st in same sc, rep from * around, join in first sc. Fasten off. Weave in ends.

15. SIMPLE 12-PETAL DAISY MEDIUM: TRADITIONAL & UPDATED

SKILL LEVEL

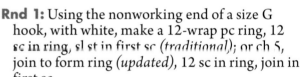

INTERMEDIATE

FINISHED MEASUREMENT
2¼ inches across

MATERIALS
- Size 10 crochet cotton:
    15 yds white
- Size 7/1.65mm steel crochet hook
- Size G/6/4mm crochet hook for pc

Rnd 1: Using the nonworking end of a size G hook, with white, make a 12-wrap pc ring, 12 sc in ring, sl st in first sc (*traditional*); or ch 5, join to form ring (*updated*), 12 sc in ring, join in first sc.

Rnd 2: Ch 1, sc in same sc, ch 7, sc in 2nd ch from hook, hdc in next ch st, dc in each of next 2 ch sts, hdc in next ch st, sc in next ch st, sl st in same sc in ring, *sc in next sc, ch 7, sc in 2nd ch from hook, hdc in next ch st, dc in each of next 2 ch sts, hdc in next ch st, sc in next ch st, sl st in same sc, rep from * around, join in first sc.

Rnd 3: Sl st in the back lp of first ch of ch-7 on next petal, ch 1, sc in same st, [ch 1, sc in back lp on next ch st] 5 times, ch 1, sc in turning ch, (ch 1, sc in same ch st) twice, ch 1, sc in next sc, ch 1, sc in next hdc, [ch 1, sc in next dc] twice, ch 1, sc in next hdc, ch 1, sc in next sc, *sc in back lp of first ch st on next petal, [ch 1, sc in back lp of next ch st] 5 times, ch 1, sc in turning ch, (ch 1, sc in same ch st) twice, ch 1, sc in next sc, ch 1, sc in next hdc, [ch 1, sc in next dc] twice, ch 1, sc in next hdc, ch 1, sc in next sc, rep from * around, join in first sc. Fasten off. Weave in ends.

16. CARNATION: TRADITIONAL & UPDATED

SKILL LEVEL

INTERMEDIATE

FINISHED MEASUREMENT
2 inches across

MATERIALS

- Size 10 crochet cotton:
  30 yds white
- Size 7/1.65mm steel crochet hook
- Size G/6/4mm crochet hook for pc

Rnd 1: Using the nonworking end of a size G hook, with white, make a 12-wrap pc ring, 16 sc in ring, sl st in first sc *(traditional)*; or ch 5, join to form ring *(updated)*, 16 sc in ring, join in first sc.

Rnd 2: Ch 3 *(counts as first dc and ch-1)*, dc in next sc, [ch 1, dc in next sc] around, ending with ch 1, join in 2nd ch of beg ch-3.

Rnd 3: Sl st in ch-1 sp, ch 1, 2 sc in same sp, [2 sc in next ch-1 sp] around, join in front lp of first sc.

Rnd 4: Working in front lp of each st, ch 1, sc in same sc, ch 5, sc in same sc, *ch 5, sc in next sc, ch 5, sc in same sc, rep from * around, ending with ch 5, join in first sc.

Rnd 5: Sl st in back lp of first sc on rnd 3, working in back lp, ch 1, sc in same sc, sc in each sc around, join in front lp of first sc.

Rnd 6: Rep rnd 4.

Rnd 7: Working in back lp of rnd 5, ch 1, sc in same sc, sc in each sc around, join in front lp of first sc.

Rnd 8: Rep rnd 4. Fasten off. Weave in ends.

17. DAISY: PC & PR

SKILL LEVEL

INTERMEDIATE

FINISHED MEASUREMENT
1¾ inches across

MATERIALS
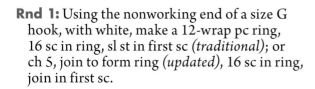
- Size 10 crochet cotton:
  25 yds white
- Size 7/1.65mm steel crochet hook
- Size F/5/3.75mm crochet hook for pc

Padding cord lengths: With white, cut 2 lengths of thread 5 feet long for padding cord, hold tog and fold in half, wrap on padding cord bobbin.

Rnd 1: Using nonworking end of size F hook, make 12-wrap pc ring, 12 sc in ring, join in first sc.

Petal 1: Ch 1, sc in same sc and through the fold of padding cord threads, work over all 4 strands of padding cord threads around unless otherwise noted, 8 sc worked over padding cord only, ch 1, turn, sc in each of next 8 sc and over padding cord, *(be sure to adjust padding cord frequently on this motif)*, sc in next sc on ring, turn.

Petals 2–12: [Sc in each of next 5 sc, 3 sc worked over padding cord only, ch 1, turn, sc in each of next 8 sc and over padding cord, sc in next sc on ring, turn] 11 times. Leaving 6-inch length, fasten off. Using tail, sew first and last petal tog up 5 sts. Weave in ends.

18. 6-PETAL FLOWER

SKILL LEVEL

INTERMEDIATE

FINISHED MEASUREMENT
2½ inches across

MATERIALS
- Size 10 crochet cotton:
  25 yds white
- Size 7/1.65mm steel crochet hook

With white, ch 6, sl st to form ring.

Rnd 1: Ch 2 (*counts as first dc*), 17 dc in ring, join in 2nd ch of beg ch-2.

Rnd 2: Working in front lp around, ch 1, sc in same st, ch 2, [sc in next dc, ch 2] around, join in first sc.

Rnd 3: Sl st in back lp of rnd 1, working in back lp, ch 1, sc in same st, sc in next dc, ch 10, sl st in 10th ch from hook to form ring, *sc in each of next 3 dc, ch 10, sl st in 10th ch from hook to form ring, rep from * around, ending with sc in last dc, join in first sc.

Rnd 4: Ch 1, sc in same st, sk next sc, sc in ch-10 lp, (hdc, 15 dc, hdc, sc) in same ch-10 lp, sk next sc, *sc in next sc, sc in ch-10 lp, (hdc, 15 dc, hdc, sc) in same ch-10 lp, sk next sc, rep from * around, join in first sc. Fasten off. Weave in ends.

Rnd 5: Join white in 2nd dc in any lp, ch 1, sc in same st, [ch 4, sk next 3 dc, sc in next dc, ch-3 picot in last sc made] twice, ch 4, sk next 3 dc, sc in next dc, *sc in 2nd dc on next lp, (ch 4, sk next 3 dc, sc in next dc, ch-3 picot in last sc made) twice, ch 4, sk next 3 dc, sc in next dc, rep from * around, join in first sc. Fasten off. Weave in ends.

19A. 5-PETAL FLOWER: TRADITIONAL WITH PC & PR

SKILL LEVEL

INTERMEDIATE

FINISHED MEASUREMENT
2¾ inches across

MATERIALS
- Size 10 crochet cotton:
  25 yds white
- Size 7/1.65mm steel crochet hook
- Size G/6/4mm crochet hook for pc

Padding cord lengths: With white, cut 2 lengths of thread 5 feet long for padding cord, hold tog and fold in half, wrap on padding cord bobbin.

Rnd 1: Using nonworking end of a size G hook, with white, make a 12-wrap pc ring, 15 sc in ring, join in first sc.

Rnd 2: Ch 1, *sc in each of next 3 sc, ch 11, sl st in 11th ch from hook, ch 1, working in ring just formed (sc, 3 hdc, 4 dc, 3 tr, 4 dc, 3 hdc, sc) in same ch-11 ring (*medallion made*), sl st around base of medallion, rep from * around, ending with sl st in first sc.

Rnd 3: Sl st in next sc, ch 1, sc in same sc and through the fold of the padding cord threads, work over all 4 strands of the padding cord threads around.

Petal 1: Sk next sc, sc in next sc, sc in each of next 3 hdc, ch-3 picot in last sc made, sc in each of next 3 dc, ch-3 picot in last sc made, sc in next dc, sc in each of next 2 tr, sc in same tr, ch-3 picot in last sc made, sc in same tr, sc in next tr, sc in each of next 2 dc, ch-3 picot in last sc made, sc in each of next 2 dc, sc in next hdc, ch-3 picot in last sc made, sc in each of next 2 hdc, sc in next sc, sk next sc.

Petals 2-4: Sc in next sc, sk next sc, sc in next sc, sc in each of next 3 hdc, ch 1, sl st in last picot on previous petal, ch 1, sl st in last sc made, sc in next

3 dc, ch-3 picot in last sc made, sc in next dc, sc in each of next 2 tr, sc in same tr, ch-3 picot in last sc made, sc in same tr, sc in next tr, sc in each of next 2 dc, ch-3 picot in last sc made, sc in each of next 2 dc, sc in next hdc, ch-3 picot in last sc made, sc in each of next 2 hdc, sc in next sc, sk next sc.

Petal 5: Sc in next sc, sk next sc, sc in next sc, sc in each of next 3 hdc, ch 1, sl st in last picot on previous petal, ch 1, sl st in last sc made, sc in each of next 3 dc, ch-3 picot in last sc made, sc in next dc, sc in each of next 2 tr, sc in same tr, ch-3 picot in last sc made, sc in same tr, sc in next tr, sc in each of next 2 dc, ch-3 picot in last sc made, sc in each of next 2 dc, sc in next hdc, ch 1, sl st in first picot on first petal made, ch 1, sl st in last sc made, sc in each of next 2 hdc, sc in next sc, sk next sc, join in first sc. Fasten off. Weave in ends.

19B. 5-PETAL FLOWER: UPDATED

SKILL LEVEL

INTERMEDIATE

FINISHED MEASUREMENT
2¾ inches across

MATERIALS
- Size 10 crochet cotton: 25 yds white
- Size 7/1.65mm steel crochet hook

Rnd 1: Ch 5, join to form ring, 15 sc in ring, join in back lp of first sc.

Rnd 2: Ch 1, *sc in next 3 sc, ch 11, sl st in 11th ch from hook, ch 1, working in ring just formed (sc, 3 hdc, 4 dc, 3 tr, 4 dc, 3 hdc, sc) in same ch-11 ring *(medallion made)*, sl st around base of medallion, rep from * around, ending with sl st in first sc.

Rnd 3: Sl st in next sc, ch 1, sc in same sc. *(now working on Petal)*

Petal 1: Sk next 2 sc, sc in next sc, sc in each of next 3 hdc, ch-3 picot in last sc made, sc in each of next

3 dc, ch-3 picot in last sc made, sc in next dc, sc in each of next 2 tr, sc in same tr, ch-3 picot in last sc made, sc in same tr, sc in next tr, sc in each of next 2 dc, ch-3 picot in last sc made, sc in each of next 2 dc, sc in next hdc, ch-3 picot in last sc made, sc in each of next 2 hdc, sc in next sc, sk next 2 sc.

Petals 2–4: Sc in next sc, sc in each of next 3 hdc, ch 1, sl st in last picot on previous petal, ch 1, sl st in last sc made, sc in each of next 3 dc, ch-3 picot in last sc made, sc in next dc, sc in each of next 2 tr, sc in same tr, ch-3 picot in last sc made, sc in same tr, sc in next tr, sc in each of next 2 dc, ch-3 picot in last sc made, sc in each of next 2 dc, sc in next hdc, ch-3 picot in last sc made, sc in each of next 2 hdc, sc in next sc, sk next 2 sc.

Petal 5: Sc in next sc, sc in each of next 3 hdc, ch 1, sl st in last picot on previous petal, ch 1, sl st in last sc made, sc in each of next 3 dc, ch-3 picot in last sc made, sc in next dc, sc in each of next 2 tr, sc in same tr, ch-3 picot in last sc made, sc in same tr, sc in next tr, sc in each of next 2 dc, ch-3 picot in last sc made, sc in each of next 2 dc, sc in next hdc, ch 1, sl st in first picot on first petal made, ch 1, sl st in last sc made, sc in each of next 2 hdc, sc in next sc, sk next 2 sc, join in first sc. Fasten off. Weave in ends.

20A. FLOWER WITH 8 CLOSED PETALS: TRADITIONAL WITH PC & PR

SKILL LEVEL

INTERMEDIATE

FINISHED MEASUREMENT
2⅝ inches across

MATERIALS
- Size 10 crochet cotton: 30 yds white
- Size 7/1.65mm steel crochet hook
- Size I/9/5.5mm crochet hook for pc
- Small amount of fiberfill for stuffing center ball

Padding cord lengths: With white, cut 2 lengths of thread 4 feet long for padding cord, hold tog and fold in half, wrap on padding cord bobbin.

Rnd 1: Using nonworking end of a size I hook, with white, make a 12-wrap pc ring, 16 sc in ring, join in first sc.

Rnd 2: Ch 1, sc in same sc, sc in next sc, ch 7, sc in 2nd ch from hook, hdc in each of next 4 ch sts, sc in next ch, [sc in each of next 2 sc, ch 7, sc in 2nd ch from hook, hdc in each of next 4 chs, sc in next ch] 7 times, join in first sc.

Rnd 3: Ch 1, sc in same sc, ch 1, sk next sc and first ch st, hdc in back lp of next ch st, [ch 1, dc in back lp of next ch st] 4 times, ch 1, dc in tip of point, ch 2, dc in same st, ch 1, dc in next sc, [ch 1, dc in next hdc] 3 times, ch 1, hdc in next hdc, ch 1, sk next sc, *sc in next sc, ch 1, sk next sc and first ch st, hdc in back lp of next ch st, [ch 1, dc in back lp of next ch st] 4 times, ch 1, dc in tip of point, ch 2, dc in same st, ch 1, dc in next sc, [ch 1, dc in next hdc] 3 times, ch 1, hdc in next hdc, ch 1, sk next sc, rep from * around, join in first sc.

Rnd 4: Ch 1, sc in same sc and through fold of padding cord threads, work over all 4 strands of padding cord threads around, sc in next ch-1 sp, [2 sc in next ch-1 sp] 5 times, 5 sc in next ch-2 sp, [2 sc in next ch-1 sp] 5 times, sc in next ch-1 sp, fold petal so the first ch-1 sp of petal and the last ch-1 sp are touching on the right side of piece, sl st in first and last ch-1 sp of petal, *sc in next sc between petals, sc in next ch-1 sp, [2 sc in next ch-1 sp] 5 times, 5 sc in next ch-2 sp, [2 sc in next ch-1 sp] 5 times, sc in next ch-1 sp, fold petal so first ch-1 sp of petal and last ch-1 sp are touching on the right side of piece, sl st in first and last ch-1 sp of petal, sc in next sc between petals, rep from * around, join in first sc. Fasten off. Weave in ends.

CENTER BALL
Ch 4, join to form ring.

Rnd 1: Ch 1, 12 sc in ring, join in first sc.

Rnd 2: Ch 1, 2 sc in same sc, sc in next sc, [2 sc in next sc, sc in next sc] 5 times, sl st in first sc. *(18 sc)*

Rnds 3 & 4: Ch 1, sc in each sc around, join in first sc.

Rnd 5: Ch 1, [sc dec over next 2 sc, sc in next sc, around, join in first sc. *(12 sc)*

Rnd 6: Ch 1, [sc dec over next 2 sc] around, join in first sc. Leaving 8-inch length, fasten off.

Stuff Center Ball with fiberfill. Weave rem 8-inch length between each dec st of previous rnd, gently pull up tight to close opening, sew Ball in cup formed in center of flower.

20B. FLOWER WITH 8 CLOSED PETALS: UPDATED

SKILL LEVEL

INTERMEDIATE

FINISHED MEASUREMENT
2⅝ inches across

MATERIALS
- Size 10 crochet cotton: 30 yds white
- Size 7/1.65mm steel crochet hook
- Small amount of fiberfill for stuffing center ball

Rnd 1: With white, ch 5, join to form ring, 16 sc in ring, join in first sc.

Rnd 2: Ch 1, sc in same sc, sc in next sc, ch 7, sc in 2nd ch from hook, hdc in each of next 4 ch sts, sc in next ch, [sc in each of next 2 sc, ch 7, sc in 2nd ch from hook, hdc in each of next 4 chs, sc in next ch] 7 times, join in first sc.

Rnd 3: Ch 1, sc in same sc, ch 1, sk next sc and first ch st, hdc in back lp of next ch st, [ch 1, dc in back lp of next ch st] 4 times, ch 1, dc in tip of point, ch 2, dc in same st, ch 1, dc in next sc, [ch 1, dc in next hdc] 3 times, ch 1, hdc in next hdc, ch 1, sk next sc, *sc in next sc and first ch st, hdc in back lp of next ch st, [ch 1, dc in back lp of next ch st] 4 times, ch 1, dc in tip of point, ch 2, dc in same st, ch 1, dc in next sc, [ch 1, dc in next hdc] 3 times, ch 1, hdc in next hdc, ch 1, sk next sc, rep from * around, join in first sc.

Rnd 4: Ch 1, sc in same sc, sc in next ch-1 sp, [2 sc in next ch-1 sp] 5 times, 5 sc in next ch-2 sp, [2 sc in next ch-1 sp] 5 times, sc in next ch-1 sp, fold petal so the first ch-1 sp of petal and the last ch-1 sp are touching on the right side of piece, sl st in first and last ch-1 sp of petal, *sc in next sc between petals, sc in next ch-1 sp, [2 sc in next ch-1 sp] 5 times, 5 sc in next ch-2 sp, [2 sc in next ch-1 sp] 5 times, sc in next ch-1 sp, fold petal so first ch-1 sp of petal and last ch-1 sp are touching on the right side of piece, sl st in first and last ch-1 sp of petal, sc in next sc between petals, rep from * around, join in first sc. Fasten off. Weave in ends.

CENTER BALL
Ch 4, join to form ring.

Rnds 1–6: Rep rnds 1–6 of Center Ball of previous traditional flower.

Stuff Center Ball with fiberfill. Weave rem 8-inch length between each dec st of previous rnd, gently pull up tight to close opening, sew Ball in cup formed in center of flower.

21A. 8-PETAL FLOWER WITH OPEN PETALS: TRADITIONAL WITH PC & PR

SKILL LEVEL

INTERMEDIATE

FINISHED MEASUREMENT
3 inches across

MATERIALS
- Size 10 crochet cotton:
  20 yds white
- Size 7/1.65mm steel crochet hook
- Size I/9/5.5mm crochet hook for pc

Padding cord lengths: With white, cut 2 lengths of thread 5 feet long for padding cord, hold 2 lengths tog and fold in half, wrap on padding cord bobbin.

Rnd 1: Using nonworking end of a size I hook, with white, make a 12-wrap pc ring, 24 sc in ring, join in first sc.

Rnd 2: Ch 1, 2 sc in same sc, sc in each of next 2 sc, [2 sc in next sc, sc in each of next 2 sc] around, join in first sc. *(32 sc)*

Rnd 3: Ch 1, sc in same sc, sc in next sc, ch 11, dc in 6th ch from hook, [ch 1, sk next ch, tr in next ch] twice, ch 1, sk next sc, *sc in each of next 3 sc, ch 11, dc in 6th ch from hook, [ch 1, sk next ch, tr in next ch] twice, ch 1, sk next sc, rep from * around, ending with sc in next sc, join in first sc.

Rnd 4: Ch 1, sc in same sc and through fold of the padding cord threads, work over all 4 strands of the padding cord threads around, sc in next ch-1 sp, ch-3 picot in last sc made, sc in same sp, [2 sc in next ch-1 sp] twice, 9 sc in next ch-5 sp, [2 sc in next ch-1 sp] twice, sc in next ch-1 sp, ch-3 picot in last sc made, sc in same sp, sk next sc, *sc in next sc, sc in next ch-1 sp, ch-3 picot in last sc made, sc in same sp, [2 sc in next ch-1 sp] twice, 9 sc in next ch-5 sp, [2 sc in next ch-1 sp] twice, sc in next ch-1 sp, ch-3 picot in last sc made, sc in same sp, sk next sc, rep from* around, join in first sc. Fasten off. Weave in ends.

Rnd 5: Join white in first sc of last ch-1 sp before tip of any petal, working up the side of petal, ch 1, sc in same sc and through the fold of the padding cord threads, work over all 4 strands of the padding cord threads around, sc in each of next 5 sc, 3 sc in next sc, sc in each of next 7 sc, *sc in 2nd sc of the 2nd ch-1 sp on next petal, sc in each of next 6 sc, 3 sc in next sc, sc in each of next 7 sc, rep from * around, ending with sc in the 2nd sc of the 2nd ch-1 sp on first petal, join in first sc. Fasten off. Weave in ends.

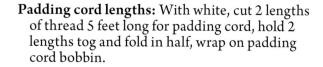

21B. 8-PETAL FLOWER WITH OPEN PETALS: UPDATED

SKILL LEVEL

INTERMEDIATE

FINISHED MEASUREMENT

3 inches across

MATERIALS

- Size 10 crochet cotton:
    20 yds white
- Size 7/1.65mm steel crochet hook

Rnd 1: With white, ch 8, join to form ring, 24 sc in ring, join in first sc.

Rnd 2: Ch 1, 2 sc in same sc, sc in each of next 2 sc, [2 sc in next sc, sc in each of next 2 sc] around, join in first sc. *(32 sc)*

Rnd 3: Ch 1, sc in same sc, sc in next sc, ch 11, dc in 6th ch from hook, [ch 1, sk next ch, tr in next ch] twice, ch 1, sk next sc, *sc in each of next 3 sc, ch 11, dc in 6th ch from hook, [ch 1, sk next ch, tr in next ch] twice, ch 1, sk next sc, rep from * around, ending with sc in next sc, join in first sc.

Rnd 4: Ch 1, sc in same sc, sc in next ch-1 sp, ch-3 picot in last sc made, sc in same sp, [2 sc in next ch-1 sp] twice, 9 sc in next ch-5 sp, [2 sc in next ch-1 sp] twice, sc in next ch-1 sp, ch-3 picot in last sc made, sc in same sp, sk next sc, *sc in next sc, sc in next ch-1 sp, ch-3 picot in last sc made, sc in same sp, [2 sc in next ch-1 sp] twice, 9 sc in next ch-5 sp, [2 sc in next ch-1 sp] twice, sc in next ch-1 sp, ch-3 picot in last sc made, sc in same sp, sk next sc, rep from * around, join in first sc. Fasten off. Weave in ends.

Rnd 5: Join white in first sc of last ch-1 sp before tip of any petal, working up the side of petal, ch 1, sc in same sc, sc in each of next 5 sc, 3 sc in next sc, sc in each of next 7 sc, *sc in 2nd sc of the 2nd ch-1 sp on next petal, sc in each of next 6 sc, 3 sc in next sc, sc in each of next 7 sc, rep from * around, ending with sc in the 2nd sc of the 2nd ch-1 sp on first petal, join in first sc. Fasten off. Weave in ends.

22. BULLION STITCH BUD PR

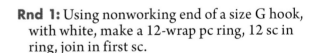

SKILL LEVEL

INTERMEDIATE

FINISHED MEASUREMENT

1⅞ inches tall

MATERIALS

- Size 10 crochet cotton:
    10 yds white
- Size 7/1.65mm steel crochet hook
- Size G/6/4mm crochet hook for pc

Rnd 1: Using nonworking end of a size G hook, with white, make a 12-wrap pc ring, 12 sc in ring, join in first sc.

Rnd 2: Ch 1, sc in same sc, sc in each of next 3 sc, ch 6, sc in 2nd ch from hook, sc in each of next 4 ch sts, sc in same sc, sc in each of next 4 sc, ch 2, 8 wrap bullion st in same sc, 8 wrap bullion st in each of next 4 sc, dc in first sc at beg of rnd, turn.

Row 1: Now working in rows, ch 4 *(counts as first dtr)*, holding the last lp of each st on the hook dtr between dc and first bullion st, [dtr between next 2 bullion sts] 4 times, dtr between last bullion st and next dc, yo, draw through all lps on hook, ch 4, sl st in top of cl just made *(for picot)*. Fasten off. Weave in end.

23. BULLION STITCH FLOWER PR

SKILL LEVEL

▰▰▰▱
INTERMEDIATE

FINISHED MEASUREMENTS

3 inches wide x 2½ inches tall

MATERIALS

- Size 10 crochet cotton:
  20 yds white
- Size 7/1.65mm steel crochet hook
- Size G/6/4mm crochet hook for pc

Rnd 1: Using nonworking end of a size G hook, with white, make a 12-wrap pc ring, 16 sc in ring, join in first sc.

Rnd 2: Ch 1, sc in same sc, sc in each of next 3 sc, ch 8, sc in 2nd ch from hook, sc in each of next 6 ch sts, sc in same sc, sc in each of next 4 sc, ch 2, 8 wrap bullion st in same sc, 8 wrap bullion st in each of next 8 sc, dc in first sc at beg of rnd, turn.

Row 1: Now working in rows, ch 1, sc in dc, [2 sc in sp between next 2 bullion sts] 8 times, sc in 2nd ch of ch-2 on previous rnd, turn.

Row 2: Ch 4, working in back lp across, holding the last lp of each st on the hook, 2 dtr in each of next 2 sc, yo, draw through all lps on hook, ch 4 picot in top of cl just made, ch 5, [sc in next sc, ch 4, holding last lp of each st on the hook, 2 dtr in each of next 3 sc, yo, draw through all lps on hook, ch 4 picot in top of cl just made, ch 5] 3 times, sc in next sc, ch 4, holding last lp of each st on the hook, 2 dtr in each of next 2 sc, yo, draw through all lps on hook, ch 4 picot in top of cl just made, ch 5, sc in last sc. Fasten off. Weave in ends.

24A. 5-PETAL MEDIUM FLOWER: TRADITIONAL WITH PC & PR

SKILL LEVEL

▰▰▰▰
EXPERIENCED

FINISHED MEASUREMENT

3½ inches across

MATERIALS

- Size 10 crochet cotton:
  25 yds white
- Size 7/1.65mm steel crochet hook
- Size J/10/6mm crochet hook for pc

Padding cord lengths: With white, cut 2 lengths of thread 5 feet long for padding cord, hold tog and fold in half, wrap on padding cord bobbin.

Rnd 1: Using nonworking end of a size J hook, with white, make a 12-wrap pc ring, 20 sc in ring, join in first sc.

Rnd 2: Working in front lp around, ch 1, sc in same sp, ch-3 picot in sc made, [sc in next sc, ch-3 picot in last sc made] around, join in first sc.

Rnd 3: Sl st in back lp of first sc of rnd 1, working in back lp around, ch 1, sc in same st and through fold of the padding cord threads, work over all 4 strands of the padding cord threads around unless otherwise indicated, sc in next sc, sl st in next sc, 23 sc over padding cord only, sl st in same sc, adjust padding cord, making sure not to pull too tight, *sc in each of next 3 sc, sl st in next sc, 23 sc over padding cord only, sl st in same sc, adjust padding cord, rep from * around, ending with a sc in last sc, join in first sc.

Rnd 4: Ch 1, sc in same sc, do not work over padding cord from this point on this rnd, sl st in next sc, ch 4, dc in 5th sc on padding cord lp, [ch 3, sk 1 sc, dc in next sc] 7 times, ch 4, sk next 4 sc, *sl st in next sc, sc in next sc, sl st in next sc, ch 4, dc in 5th sc on padding cord lp, [ch 3, sk 1 sc, dc in next sc] 7 times, ch 4, sk next 4 sc, rep from * around, ending with sl st in last sc of rnd, join in first sc.

Rnd 5 (Petal 1): Pick up padding cord, work over all 4 strands of the padding cord threads around unless otherwise indicated, 5 sc in next ch-4 sp, 4 sc in next ch-3 sp, [2 sc in next ch-3 sp, ch-3 picot in last sc made, 2 sc in same sp] 5 times, 4 sc in next ch-3 sp, 5 sc in next ch-4 sp, sl st in next sc.

Petals 2–4: 5 sc in next ch-4 sp, sl st in the 5th sc of last ch-4 sp on previous petal, 4 sc in next ch-3 sp, [2 sc in next ch-3 sp, ch-3 picot in last sc made, 2 sc in same sp] 5 times, 4 sc in next ch-3 sp, 5 sc in next ch-4 sp, sl st in next sc.

Petal 5: 5 sc in next ch-4 sp, sl st in the 5th sc of last ch-4 sp on previous petal, 4 sc in next ch-3 sp, [2 sc in next ch-3 sp, ch-3 picot in last sc made, 2 sc in same sp] 5 times, 4 sc in next ch-3 sp, sl st in the 5th sc worked in first ch-4 sp on first petal, 5 sc in next ch-4 sp on 5th petal, join in first sc. Fasten off. Weave in ends.

24B. 5-PETAL MEDIUM FLOWER: UPDATED

SKILL LEVEL

INTERMEDIATE

FINISHED MEASUREMENTS
3½ inches across

MATERIALS
- Size 10 crochet cotton:
  25 yds white
- Size 7/1.65mm steel crochet hook

Ch 7, join to form ring.

Rnd 1: Ch 1, 20 sc in ring, sl st in front lp of first sc.

Rnd 2: Working in front lp around, ch 1, sc in same sc, ch 3, picot in top of last sc made, [sc in next sc, ch-3 picot in last sc made] around, join in first sc.

Rnd 3: Sl st in back lp of first sc of rnd 1, sc in each of next 2 sc, ch 12, sl st in 12th ch from hook to form ring, 23 sc in ring, sl st around base of ring, [sc in each of next 4 sc, ch 12, sl st in 12th ch from hook to form ring, 23 sc in ring, sl st around base of ring] 4 times, ending with a sc in next sc, join in first sc.

Rnd 4: Ch 1, sc in same sc, sl st in next sc, ch 4, dc in 5th sc of 23-sc ring, [ch 3, sk 1 sc, dc in next sc] 7 times, ch 4, sk next 4 sc, *sl st in next sc, sc in next sc, sl st in next sc, ch 4, dc in 5th sc of 23-sc ring, [ch 3, sk 1 sc, dc in next sc] 7 times, ch 4, sk next 4 sc, rep from * around, ending with sl st in last sc of rnd, join in first sc.

Rnd 5 (Petal 1): 5 sc in next ch-4 sp, 4 sc in next ch-3 sp, [2 sc in next ch-3 sp, ch-3 picot in last sc made, 2 sc in same sp] 5 times, 4 sc in next ch-3 sp, 5 sc in next ch-4 sp, sl st in next sc.

Petals 2–4: 5 sc in next ch-4 sp, 4 sc in next ch-3 sp, [2 sc in next ch-3 sp, ch-3 picot in last sc made, 2 sc in same sp] 5 times, 4 sc in next ch-3 sp, 5 sc in next ch-4 sp, sl st in next sc.

Petal 5: 5 sc in next ch-4 sp, sl st in the 5th sc of last ch-4 sp on previous petal, 4 sc in next ch-3 sp, [2 sc in next ch-3 sp, ch-3 picot in last sc made, 2 sc in same sp] 5 times, 4 sc in next ch-3 sp, sl st in the next sc of ch-4 sp on first petal, 5 sc in next ch-4 sp on 5th petal, join in first sc. Fasten off. Weave in ends.

25A. 6-PETAL FLOWER WITH CLUSTERS: TRADITIONAL WITH PC & PR

SKILL LEVEL

INTERMEDIATE

FINISHED MEASUREMENT
3 inches across

MATERIALS
- Size 10 crochet cotton:
  35 yds white
- Size 7/1.65mm steel crochet hook
- Size I/9/5.5mm crochet hook for pc

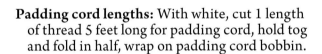

Padding cord lengths: With white, cut 1 length of thread 5 feet long for padding cord, hold tog and fold in half, wrap on padding cord bobbin.

Rnd 1: Using nonworking end of a size I hook, with white, make a 12-wrap pc ring, 18 sc in ring, join in first sc.

Rnd 2: Ch 5 (*counts as first tr, ch 2*), working in back lp, [tr in next sc, ch 2] rep around, join in 3rd ch of beg ch-5. (*18 tr, 18 ch-2 sps*)

Rnd 3: Ch 1, sc in same st, 2 sc in next ch-2 sp, [sc in next tr, 2 sc in next ch-2 sp] around, join in first sc. (*54 sc*)

PETAL 1
Row 1: Sl st in 2nd sc of previous rnd, ch 1, sc in same sc, sc in each of next 6 sc, turn. (*7 sc*)

Row 2: Ch 1, sc in each of next 6 sc, 2 sc in next sc, turn. (*8 sc*)

Row 3: Ch 1, sc in each of next 4 sc, holding last lp of each st on the hook, 4 fpdc cl in 4th sc on row 1 of petal, yo, draw through all lps on hook, sc in each of next 4 sc on row 2, turn. (*8 sc, 1 fpdc cl*)

Row 4: Ch 1, sc in each of next 4 sc, sc in top of 4-fpdc cl, sc in each of next 4 sc, turn. (*9 sc*)

Row 5: Ch 1, sc in each of next 2 sc, work 4 fpdc cl in 3rd sc on row 3, sk sc behind fpdc cl, sc in each of next 3 sc, 4 fpdc cl in 7th st on row 3, sk sc behind fpdc cl, sc in each of next 2 sc, turn. (*7 sc, 2 fpdc cls*)

Row 6: Ch 1, sc in each of next 2 sc, sc in next fpdc cl, sc in each of next 3 sc, sc in next fpdc cl, sc in each of next 2 sc, turn. (*9 sc*)

Row 7: Ch 1, sc in each of next 4 sc, fpdc cl in 5th st on row 5, sk sc behind fpdc cl, sc in each of next 4 sc, turn. (*8 sc, 1 fpdc cl*)

Row 8: Ch 1, sc dec in next 2 sc, sc in each of next 2 sc, sc in top of next fpdc cl, sc in each of next 2 sc, sc dec in last 2 sc. Fasten off. Weave in ends. (*7 sc*)

PETALS 2-6
Row 1: Sk next 2 sc of rnd 3, join white in next sc, ch 1, sc in same sc, sc in each of next 6 sc, turn. (*7 sc*)

Rows 2-8: Rep rows 2-8 of Petal 1. After 6th petal is completed, **do not fasten off, turn.**

EDGING
Ch 1, sc in first sc of row 8 and through the fold of the padding cord thread, working over both strands of the padding cord, sc in each of next 5 sc, 2 sc in next sc, sc in end of each of the next 7 rows down side of Petal, sk next sc of rnd 3, sc in next sc, sk next sc of rnd 3, sc in end of each of the next 7 rows up the side of Petal, sc in first sc of row 8, drop padding cord, ch 5, turn, sc in the first sc on end of previous petal, sl st in next sc, turn, 2 sc over ch-5, ch-3 picot in last sc made, 4 sc over same ch-5, ch-3 picot in last sc made, 2 sc over same ch-5, *pick up padding cord, 2 sc in first sc on row 8, sc in each of next 5 sc, 2 sc in next sc, sc in end of each of the next 7 rows down the side of the Petal, sk next sc of rnd 3, sc in next sc, sk next sc of rnd 3, sc in end of each of the next 7 rows up side of Petal, sc in first sc of row 8, drop pc, ch 5, turn, sc in first sc on the end of previous petal, sl st in next sc, turn, 2 sc over ch-5, ch-3 picot in last sc made, 4 sc over same ch-5, ch-3 picot in last sc made, 2 sc over same ch-5, rep from * around, ending with sc in same sc as first sc, join in first sc. Fasten off. Weave in ends.

25B. 6-PETAL FLOWER WITH CLUSTERS: UPDATED

SKILL LEVEL

INTERMEDIATE

FINISHED MEASUREMENT

3⅛ inches across

MATERIALS

- Size 10 crochet cotton:
  35 yds white
- Size 7/1.65mm steel crochet hook

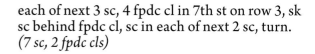

Rnd 1: Ch 6, join to form ring, 18 sc in ring, join in first sc.

Rnd 2: Ch 5 *(counts as first tr, ch 2)*, working in back lp, [tr in next sc, ch 2] rep around, ending with sl st in 3rd ch of beg ch-5.

Rnd 3: Ch 1, sc in same st, 2 sc in next ch-2 sp, [sc in next tr, 2 sc in next ch-2 sp] around, join in first sc. *(54 sc)*

PETAL 1

Row 1: Sl st in 2nd sc of previous rnd, ch 1, sc in same sc, sc in each of next 6 sc, turn. *(7 sc)*

Row 2: Ch 1, sc in each of next 6 sc, 2 sc in next sc, turn. *(8 sc)*

Row 3: Ch 1, sc in each of next 4 sc, holding last lp of each st on the hook, 4 fpdc cl in 4th sc on row 1 of petal, yo, draw through all lps on hook, sc in each of next 4 sc on row 2, turn. *(8 sc, 1 fpdc cl)*

Row 4: Ch 1, sc in each of next 4 sc, sc in top of 4-fpdc cl, sc in each of next 4 sc, turn. *(9 sc)*

Row 5: Ch 1, sc in each of next 2 sc, work 4 fpdc cl in 3rd sc on row 3, sk sc behind fpdc cl, sc in

each of next 3 sc, 4 fpdc cl in 7th st on row 3, sk sc behind fpdc cl, sc in each of next 2 sc, turn. *(7 sc, 2 fpdc cls)*

Row 6: Ch 1, sc in each of next 2 sc, sc in next fpdc cl, sc in each of next 3 sc, sc in next fpdc cl, sc in each of next 2 sc, turn. *(9 sc)*

Row 7: Ch 1, sc in next 4 sc, fpdc cl in 5th st on row 5, sk sc behind fpdc cl, sc in each of next 4 sc, turn. *(8 sc, 1 fpdc cl)*

Row 8: Ch 1, sc dec in next 2 sc, sc in each of next 2 sc, sc in top of next fpdc cl, sc in each of next 2 sc, sc dec in last 2 sc. Fasten off. Weave in ends. *(7 sc)*

PETALS 2–6

Row 1: Sk next 2 sc of rnd 3, join white in next sc, ch 1, sc in same sc, sc in each of next 6 sc, turn. *(7 sc)*

Rows 2–8: Rep rows 2–8 of Petal 1. After 6th petal is completed, **do not fasten off, turn.**

EDGING

Ch 1, sc in first sc, sc in each of next 5 sc, 2 sc in next sc, sc in end of each of the next 7 rows down side of Petal, sk next sc of rnd 3, sc in next sc, sk next sc of rnd 3, sc in end of each of the next 7 rows up the side of Petal, sc in first sc of row 8, ch 5, turn, sc in the first sc on end of previous petal, sl st in next sc, turn, 2 sc over ch-5, ch-3 picot in last sc made, 4 sc over same ch-5, ch-3 picot in last sc made, 2 sc over same ch-5, *2 sc in first sc on row 8, sc in each of next 5 sc, 2 sc in next sc, sc in end of each of next 7 rows down the side of the Petal, sk next sc of rnd 3, sc in next sc, sk next sc of rnd 3, sc in end of each of next 7 rows up the side of Petal, sc in first sc of row 8, ch 5, turn, sc in first sc on the end of previous petal, sl st in next sc, turn, 2 sc over ch-5, ch-3 picot in last sc made, 4 sc over same ch-5, ch-3 picot in last sc made, 2 sc over same ch-5, rep from * around, ending with sc in same sc as first sc, join in first sc. Fasten off. Weave in ends. ▪

Chapter 3 LEAVES

You can't have flowers without leaves to set them off. I have provided a wide variety of sizes, shapes and styles to give you the most options—from very simple techniques to more complex patterns.

1. SMALL 2-LEAF SPRAY

SKILL LEVEL

EASY

FINISHED MEASUREMENTS

¾ inch wide x 1⅛ inches long

MATERIALS
- Size 10 crochet cotton: 5 yds white
- Size 7/1.65mm steel crochet hook

LACE

Row 1: Ch 10, holding the last lp of each st on the hook, 2 tr in 4th ch from hook (*3 sk chs count as first tr*), yo, draw through all lps on hook, ch 2, sl st in top of cl just made, ch 4, sl st in ch at base of leaf, sl st in next 3 ch sts, ch 3, holding the last lp of each st on the hook, 2 tr in same ch, yo, draw through all lps on hook, ch 2, sl st in top of cl just made, ch 4, sl st in same ch at base of leaf, sl st in next 2 chs. Fasten off. Weave in ends.

2. SIMPLE LEAF

SKILL LEVEL

EASY

FINISHED MEASUREMENTS

⅝ inch wide x 1⅛ inches long

MATERIALS
- Size 10 crochet cotton: 5 yds white
- Size 7/1.65mm steel crochet hook

LACE

Row 1: Ch 7, 2 sc in 2nd ch from hook, ch-3 picot in last sc made, hdc in each of next 2 chs, 3 dc in next ch st, hdc in next ch, 2 sc in next ch, ch 4, sl st in 2nd ch from hook, sl st in next 2 chs, sc in same ch as last 2 sc worked on opposite side of foundation ch, hdc in next ch, 3 dc in next ch, hdc in each of next 2 chs, join in first sc. Fasten off. Weave in ends.

3A. LEAF WITH PICOTS: TRADITIONAL

SKILL LEVEL

INTERMEDIATE

FINISHED MEASUREMENTS

1 inch wide x 1⅝ inches long

MATERIALS
- Size 10 crochet cotton: 10 yds white
- Size 7/1.65mm steel crochet hook

LACE

Padding cord lengths: Cut 2 lengths of white thread 24 inches long for padding cord, hold tog and fold in half, wrap on padding cord bobbin.

Rnd 1: Ch 10, 2 sc in 2nd ch from hook, hdc in next ch, dc in each of next 5 chs, hdc in next ch st, 3 sc in next ch, working on opposite side of foundation ch, hdc in next ch, dc in each of next 5 chs, hdc in next ch, sc in next ch, ending with sl st in first sc.

Rnd 2: Ch 1, sc in same sc and through the fold of the padding cord threads, work over all 4 strands of the padding cord threads around, ch-3 picot in last sc made, sc in same sc, sc in next sc, sc in next hdc, ch-3 picot in last sc made, sc in each of next 3 dc, ch-3 picot in last sc made, sc in each of next 2 dc, sc in next hdc, ch-3 picot in last sc made, sc in each of next 2 sc, drop padding cord, ch 6, sc in 2nd ch from hook, sc in each of next 4 chs, pick up padding cord, sc in same sc, sc in next sc, sc in next hdc, ch-3 picot in last sc made, sc in each of next 3 dc, ch-3 picot in last sc made, sc in each of next 2 dc, sc in next hdc, ch-3 picot in last sc made, sc in next sc, join in first sc. Fasten off. Weave in ends.

3B. LEAF WITH PICOTS: UPDATED

SKILL LEVEL

EASY

FINISHED MEASUREMENTS

1 inch wide x 2 inches long

MATERIALS

- Size 10 crochet cotton: 10 yds white
- Size 7/1.65mm steel crochet hook

Rnd 1: Ch 10, 2 sc in 2nd ch from hook, hdc in next ch, dc in each of next 5 chs, hdc in next ch, 3 sc in next ch, working on opposite side of foundation ch, hdc in next ch, dc in each of next 5 chs, hdc in next ch, sc in next ch, ending with sl st in first sc.

Rnd 2: Ch 1, sc in same sc, ch-3 picot in last sc made, sc in same sc, sc in next sc, sc in next hdc, ch-3 picot in last sc made, sc in each of next 3 dc, ch-3 picot in last sc made, sc in each of next 2 dc, sc in next hdc, ch-3 picot in last sc made, sc in each of next 2 sc, ch 6, sc in 2nd ch from hook, sc in next 4 chs, sc in same sc, sc in next sc, sc in next hdc, ch-3 picot in last sc made, sc in each of next 3 dc, ch-3 picot in last sc made, sc in each of next 2 dc, sc in next hdc, ch-3 picot in last sc made, sc in next sc, join in first sc. Fasten off. Weave in ends.

4. DOUBLE CROCHET LEAF

SKILL LEVEL

EASY

FINISHED MEASUREMENTS

1¾ inches wide x 2¾ inches long

MATERIALS

- Size 10 crochet cotton: 20 yds white
- Size 7/1.65mm steel crochet hook

Ch 13, sc in 2nd ch from hook, hdc in next ch, dc in each of next 9 ch sts, 7 dc in next ch, working on opposite side of foundation ch, dc in each of next 8 chs, ch 2, picot in top of last dc made, turn, sl st up to and in 4th dc, ch 4, sl st in the 3rd ch from hook, dc in each of next 7 dc, 7 dc in next dc, dc in each of next 11 dc, ch 2 picot in last dc made, turn, sl st up to and in 4th dc, ch 4, sl st in 3rd ch from hook, dc in each of next 10 dc, 7 dc in next dc, dc in each of next 8 dc, ch 2 picot in last dc made, sl st up to and in the 11th dc, ch 6, sc in 2nd ch from hook, sc in each of next 4 ch sts, sl st in same dc, sc in next dc, hdc in each of next 2 dc, dc in each of next 8 dc, ch 2 picot in last dc made. Fasten off. Weave in ends.

5. CLASSIC LEAF A & B

SKILL LEVEL

INTERMEDIATE

FINISHED MEASUREMENTS

A. 1¾ inches wide x 2¼ inches long

B. 1¾ inches wide x 2⅞ inches long

MATERIALS

- Size 10 crochet cotton:
  20 yds white
- Size 7/1.65mm steel crochet hook

Ch 9, sc in 2nd ch from hook, sc in each ch to
end, ch 3, sc in each st on opposite side of the
ch for 7 sts, ch 2, turn, sc in 2nd ch from hook,
working in back lp, sc in each of next 7 sc, (sc,
ch 3, sc) in ch-3 lp, working up opposite side
of leaf in back lp, sc in each of next 7 sc, *ch 2,
turn, sc in 2nd ch from hook, working in back
lp, sc in each of next 8 sc, (sc, ch 3, sc) in ch-3
lp, working up opposite side of leaf in back lp,
sc in each of next 7 sc, rep from * until you have
one center point and 5 side points on 1 side and
are up to the 5th point on last side, ch 2, turn,

sc in 2nd ch from hook, working in back lp, sc
in each of next 8 sc, sc in ch-3 lp, Fasten off here
or work:

Optional stem: Ch 6, turn, sc in 2nd ch from
hook, sc in each of next 4 chs, sc in ch-3 sp on
leaf, fasten off here or;

Optional overstitching: Sl st up center of leaf to
create an over st on spine of the Leaf. Fasten
off. Weave in ends.

Leaf can be made with as many points as desired
by just doing the rep as many times as needed
or desired.

Leaf can also be made larger or smaller by the
number of starting chains used, adjusting sc
sts to fit. Example: With a starting ch of 11,
you would work 9 sc up the opposite side of
foundation ch.

6. LEAF WITH PADDING CORD

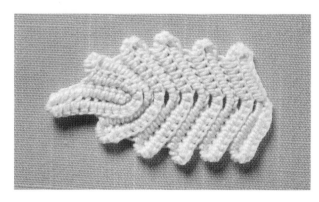

SKILL LEVEL

INTERMEDIATE

FINISHED MEASUREMENTS

1¼ inches wide x 2½ inches long

MATERIALS

- Size 10 crochet cotton:
  25 yds white
- Size 7/1.65mm steel crochet hook

Padding cord lengths: Cut 2 lengths of white
thread 5 feet long for padding cord, hold tog
and fold in half, wrap on pc bobbin.

Ch 9, sc in 2nd ch from hook and through fold of padding cord, working over all 4 strands of padding cord, sc in each of next 7 chs, 3 sc over padding cord only, working in back lp of foundation ch, sc in each of next 8 chs, 3 sc over padding cord only, working in back lp from here on, sc in each of next 6 sc, working up side of leaf, 3 sc over padding cord only, turn, sk 3 sc on padding cord and next sc on side of leaf, sc in each of next 6 sc, *3 sc over padding cord only, sk next sc, sc in each of next 6 sc on next side of leaf, 3 sc over padding cord only, turn, sk 3 sc on padding cord and next sc on side of leaf, sc in each of next 6 sc, rep from * until you have one center point and 5 points on each side of the leaf, ending with join in next sc. Fasten off. Weave in ends. You can work more reps for larger leaf.

7A. OPEN LEAF: TRADITIONAL

SKILL LEVEL

INTERMEDIATE

FINISHED MEASUREMENTS

1 inch wide x 2⅛ inches long

MATERIALS

- Size 10 crochet cotton:
  20 yds white
- Size 7/1.65mm steel crochet hook

Padding cord lengths: Cut 2 lengths of white thread 3 feet long for padding cord, hold tog and fold in half, wrap on pc bobbin.

Rnd 1: Ch 18, hdc in the 4th ch from hook, ch 1, sk next ch, dc in next ch st, [ch 1, sk next ch, tr in next ch] 3 times, ch 1, sk next ch, dc in next ch, ch 1, sk next ch, hdc in next ch, ch 1, sk next ch, join in next ch.

Rnd 2: Ch 1, sc in same sp and through the fold of the padding cord threads, work over all 4 strands of the padding cord threads around, 3 sc in same sp, [3 sc in next ch-1 sp] 6 times, 7 sc in next ch sp, [3 sc in next ch-1 sp] 6 times, 3 sc in next ch sp, join in first sc.

Rnd 3: Ch 1, working through fold of padding cord, working over all 4 strands of padding cord around, sc in same sc, ch-3 picot in last sc made, sc in same sc, sc in next sc, [ch 3, sc in each of next 2 sc] 12 times, ch 3, sc in same sc, sc in next sc, [ch 3, sc in each of next 2 sc] 11 times, ch 3, sc in next sc, join in first sc. Fasten off. Weave in ends.

7B. OPEN LEAF: UPDATED

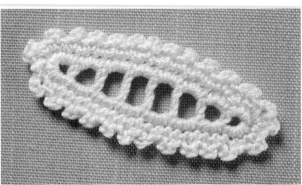

SKILL LEVEL

INTERMEDIATE

FINISHED MEASUREMENTS

1 inch wide x 2¼ inches long

MATERIALS

- Size 10 crochet cotton:
  15 yds white
- Size 7/1.65mm steel crochet hook

Rnd 1: Ch 18, hdc in the 4th ch from hook, ch 1, sk next ch, dc in next ch st, [ch 1, sk next ch, tr in next ch] 3 times, ch 1, sk next ch, dc in next ch, ch 1, sk next ch, hdc in next ch, ch 1, sk next ch, join in next ch.

Rnd 2: Ch 1, 4 sc in same sp, [3 sc in next ch-1 sp] 6 times, 7 sc in next ch sp, [3 sc in next ch-1 sp] 6 times, 3 sc in next ch sp, join in first sc.

Rnd 3: Ch 1, sc in same sc, ch-3 picot in last sc made, sc in same sc, sc in next sc, [ch 3, sc in each of next 2 sc] 12 times, ch 3, sc in same sc, sc in next sc, [ch 3, sc in each of next 2 sc] 11 times, ch 3, sc in next sc, join in first sc. Fasten off. Weave in ends.

8A. OPEN EDGE LEAF: TRADITIONAL

SKILL LEVEL

INTERMEDIATE

FINISHED MEASUREMENTS
1½ inches wide x 2⅝ inches long

MATERIALS
- Size 10 crochet cotton:
  15 yds white
- Size 7/1.65mm steel crochet hook

Padding cord lengths: Cut 2 lengths of white thread each 12 inches long for padding cord, hold tog and fold in half.

Rnd 1: Ch 10, 2 sc in 2nd ch from hook, dc in each of next 7 chs, 3 sc in next ch, working on opposite side of foundation ch, dc in each of next 7 chs, sc in next ch st, sl st in first sc.

Rnd 2: Ch 5 (*counts as first dc, ch 3*), dc in same sc, ch 3, dc in next dc, [ch 3, sk next dc, dc in next dc] 3 times, ch 3, sk next sc, dc in next sc, ch 3, dc in same sc, ch 3, dc in next dc, [ch 3, sk

next dc, dc in next dc] 3 times, ch 3, sk next sc, dc in next sc, ch 3, join in 2nd ch of beg ch-5.

Rnd 3: Ch 5, sc in 2nd ch from hook and through the fold of padding cord threads, work over all 4 strands of the padding cord threads around, sc in each of next 3 chs (*stem*), [(sc, 3 dc, sc) in next ch-3 sp] 6 times, (sc, 5 dc, sc) in next ch-3 sp, [(sc, 3 dc, sc) in next ch-3 sp] 6 times, sl st in base of stem. Fasten off. Weave in ends.

8B. OPEN EDGE LEAF: UPDATED

SKILL LEVEL

INTERMEDIATE

FINISHED MEASUREMENTS
1½ inches wide x 2⅞ inches long

MATERIALS
- Size 10 crochet cotton:
  20 yds white
- Size 7/1.65mm steel crochet hook

Rnd 1: Ch 10, 2 sc in 2nd ch from hook, dc in each of next 7 chs, 3 sc in next ch, working on opposite side of foundation ch, dc in each of next 7 chs, sc in next ch, join in first sc.

Rnd 2: Ch 5 (*counts as first dc, ch 3*), dc in same sc, ch 3, dc in next dc, [ch 3, sk next dc, dc in next dc] 3 times, ch 3, sk next sc, dc in next sc, ch 3, dc in same sc, ch 3, dc in next dc, [ch 3, sk next dc, dc in next dc] 3 times, ch 3, sk next sc, dc in next sc, ch 3, join in 2nd ch of beg ch-5.

Rnd 3: Ch 5, sc in 2nd ch from hook, sc in each of next 3 chs (*stem*), [(sc, 3 dc, sc) in next ch-3 sp] 6 times, (sc, 5 dc, sc) in next ch-3 sp, [(sc, 3 dc, sc) in next ch-3 sp] 6 times, sl st in base of stem. Fasten off. Weave in ends.

9. LEAF

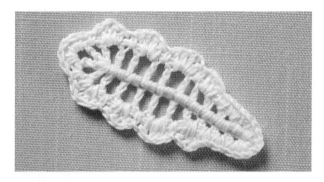

SKILL LEVEL

INTERMEDIATE

FINISHED MEASUREMENTS

1⅛ inches wide x 2½ inches long

MATERIALS

- Size 10 crochet cotton:
  15 yds white
- Size 7/1.65mm steel crochet hook

Padding cord lengths: Cut 2 lengths of white thread each 3 feet long for padding cord, hold tog and fold in half, wrap on padding cord bobbin.

Draw up a lp of white through the fold of padding cord, ch 1, work 20 sc over all 4 strands of padding cord, adjust tension of cord as needed, work over all 4 strands of padding cord unless otherwise noted throughout.

Rnd 1: Drop padding cord, ch 1, turn, sk first sc, sc in back lp of next sc, work in back lp across, [ch 1, sk next sc, sc in next sc] 3 times, ch 1, sk next sc, hdc in next sc, [ch 1, sk next sc, dc in next sc] 5 times, [ch 1, dc in end st] 4 times, ch 1, dc in rem free lp on rem side of padding cord, [ch 1, sk next sc, dc in rem free lp on rem side of padding cord] 4 times, ch 1, sk next sc, hdc in rem free lp of next sc, [ch 1, sk next sc, sc in rem free lp of next sc] 4 times ch 1, join in first sc, turn.

Rnd 2: Pick up padding cord, [2 sc in next ch-1 sp] 3 times, 3 dc in next ch-1 sp, sc in next ch-1 sp, [4 dc in next ch-1 sp, sc in next ch-1 sp] 3 times, 5 sc in next ch-1 sp, sc in next ch-1 sp, [4 dc in next ch-1 sp, sc in next ch-1 sp] 3 times, 3 dc in next ch-1 sp, [2 sc in next ch-1 sp] 4 times, join in first sc. Fasten off. Weave in ends.

10. LEAF WITH CENTER RIDGE

SKILL LEVEL

INTERMEDIATE

FINISHED MEASUREMENTS

1¼ inches wide x 3 inches long

MATERIALS

- Size 10 crochet cotton:
  15 yds white
- Size 7/1.65mm steel crochet hook

Padding cord lengths: Cut 2 lengths of white thread each 24 inches long for padding cord, hold tog and fold in half, wrap on padding cord bobbin.

Rnd 1: Ch 16, 2 sc in 2nd ch from hook ch 2, sk next ch, hdc in next ch, ch 2, sk next ch, dc in next ch, ch 2, sk next ch, tr in next ch, ch 1, sk next ch, tr in next ch, ch 2, sk next ch, dc in next ch, ch 1, sk next ch, hdc in next ch, ch 1, sk next ch, 2 sc in next ch, working on opposite side of foundation ch, ch 1, sk next ch, hdc in next ch, ch 1, sk next ch, dc in next ch, ch 2, sk next ch, tr in next ch, ch 1, sk next ch, tr in next ch, ch 2, sk next ch, dc in next ch, ch 2, sk next ch, hdc in next ch, ch 2, sk next ch, join in first sc.

Row 1: Now working in rows for center of leaf, ch 1, turn so you are working over the foundation ch sts in center of leaf, [2 sc in ch-1 sp] 7 times, ch 1, join in 2nd sc at end of leaf.

Rnd 2: Now working in rnds, ch 1, sc in same sc and fold of padding cord, work over all 4 strands of padding cord around, sc in next sc, (2 sc in next ch sp, ch-3 picot in last sc made, sc in same ch sp) 7 times, sc in next sc, 2 sc in next sc, (2 sc in next ch sp, ch-3 picot in last sc made, sc in same ch sp) 7 times, sc in next sc, sl st in next sc, 9 sc over padding cord only, drop padding cord, turn, sc over padding cord and in each sc back up to the Leaf, sl st in same sc on Leaf. Fasten off. Weave in ends.

11. LEAF

SKILL LEVEL
INTERMEDIATE

FINISHED MEASUREMENTS
1⅛ inches wide x 3 inches long

MATERIALS
- Size 10 crochet cotton:
  15 yds white
- Size 7/1.65mm steel crochet hook

Padding cord lengths: Cut 2 lengths of white thread each 24 inches long for padding cord, hold tog and fold in half, wrap on padding cord bobbin.

Row 1: Ch 17, sc in 5th ch from hook, [ch 2, sk next ch, sc in next ch] 6 times, turn.

Row 2: Sc in first ch-2 sp, [ch 2, sc in next ch-2 sp] 5 times, ch 2, sc in next ch sp, turn.

Row 3: Ch 3, sc in first ch-2 sp, [ch 2, sc in next ch-2 sp] 5 times, ch 2, sc in next sc and in fold of padding cord, work over all 4 strands of padding cord unless otherwise noted.

Rnd 1: Now working in rnds, starting on opposite side of foundation ch, 3 sc in first ch-1 sp, [2 sc in next ch-1 sp, ch-3 picot in last sc made, sc in same sp] 5 times, 2 sc in next ch sp, ch-3 picot in last sc made, sc in same sp, 3 sc over padding cord alone, ch-3 picot in last sc made, 2 sc over padding cord alone, 2 sc in next ch sp, ch-3 picot in last sc made, sc in same sp, [2 sc in next ch-2 sp, ch-3 picot in last sc made, sc in same sp] 5 times, 3 sc in next ch-2 sp, sl st in next sc, 9 sc over padding cord alone, drop padding cord, turn, working in opposite side of stem, sc over the padding cord, sc in each sc back up to the leaf, sl st in same sc on leaf. Fasten off. Weave in ends.

12. LARGE LEAF

SKILL LEVEL
EXPERIENCED

FINISHED MEASUREMENTS
2¾ inches wide x 4 inches long

MATERIALS
- Size 10 crochet cotton:
  35 yds white
- Size 7/1.65mm steel crochet hook

Padding cord lengths: Cut 2 lengths of white thread each 9 feet long for padding cord, hold tog and fold in half, wrap on padding cord bobbin.

With white, catch up thread through the fold of padding cord, ch 1, 36 sc worked over all 4 strands of padding cord, adjust tension of cord as needed, work over all four strands of padding cord unless otherwise noted throughout, turn, sc in each of next 12 sc, turn, sc in each of next 8 sc, work 4 sc over padding cord only, [turn, sc in each of next 16 sc, turn, sc in each of next 10 sc, 2 sc over padding cord only] 5 times, turn, sc in each of next 16 sc, 7 sc over padding cord only, turn, working on other side of leaf, sc over the padding cord, sc between each of the next 34 sc, 5 sc over padding cord only, drop padding cord, turn, sc in next sc, [ch 3, sk next 2 sc, sc in next sc] 4 times, ch 1, sk next 2 sc, hdc in next sc, turn, sc in same sp, [ch 3, sc in next ch-3 sp] 4 times, sl st down to the point of leaf where padding cord was dropped, pick up padding cord, turn, 2 sc in ch-1 sp, [4 sc in next ch-3 sp] 4 times, 2 sc in next ch-1 sp, sc in each of next 5 sc, (turn, sc in next 11 sc, 5 sc over padding cord only, drop padding cord, turn, sc in next sc, [ch 3, sk next 2 sc, sc in next sc] 4 times, ch 1, sk next 2 sc, hdc in next sc, turn, sc in ch sp, [ch 3, sc in next ch-3 sp] 4 times, sl st down to the point of leaf where padding cord was dropped, pick up padding cord, turn, 2 sc in ch sp, [4 sc in next ch-3 sp] 4 times, 2 sc in next ch sp, sc in each of next 5 sc) twice. Fasten off. Weave in ends.

13. FROND

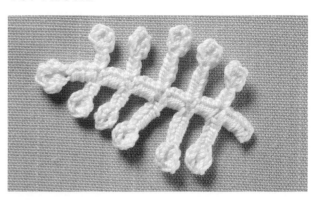

SKILL LEVEL

INTERMEDIATE

FINISHED MEASUREMENTS

1½ inches wide x 2⅛ inches long

MATERIALS

- Size 10 crochet cotton:
    15 yds white
- Size 7/1.65mm steel crochet hook

Padding cord lengths: Cut 2 lengths of white thread each 12 inches long for padding cord, hold tog and fold in half.

Ch 8, dc in 3rd ch from hook (*2 sk chs count as first dc*), ch 2, sl st in same ch, 2 sc over next ch, sc in next ch, [ch 7, 2 dc in 2nd ch from hook, ch 2, sl st in same ch, 4 sc over next 2 chs, sc in next ch] twice, [ch 6, 2 dc in 2nd ch from hook, ch 2, sl st in same ch, 2 sc over next ch st, sc in next ch st] twice, ch 4, 4 dc in 2nd ch from hook, ch 2, sl st in same ch and through fold of padding cord, working over all four strands of padding cord unless otherwise stated, 4 sc over next 2 chs, [sl st in side of sc of next stem, drop padding cord, ch 4, 2 dc in 2nd ch from hook, ch 2, sl st in same ch, 2 sc over rem chs, sl st in side of same sc on stem, working over padding cord, 4 sc over next 2 chs on stem] twice, [sl st in side of sc of next stem, drop padding cord, ch 5, 2 dc in 2nd ch from hook, ch 2, sl st in same ch, 4 sc over rem chs, sl st in side of same sc, working over padding cord, 4 sc over next 2 chs on stem] twice, sl st in side of sc of next stem, drop padding cord, ch 4, 2 dc in 2nd ch from hook, ch 2, sl st in same ch, 2 sc over rem chs, sl st in side of same sc, working over padding cord, 4 sc over all but the last ch st, sc in last ch st. Fasten off. Weave in ends.

14A. FERN

SKILL LEVEL

INTERMEDIATE

FINISHED MEASUREMENTS
2¼ inches wide x 2⅞ inches long

MATERIALS
- Size 10 crochet cotton:
  25 yds white
- Size 7/1.65mm steel crochet hook

0 LACE

FIRST LEAF & STEM
Ch 11, dc in 2nd ch from hook, ch 2, sl st in same ch (leaf nob made), ch 4, dc in 2nd ch from hook, ch 2, sl st in same ch, ch 3, 3 dc in 2nd ch from hook, ch 2, sl st in same ch, sl st in next ch, [sl st in base of nob of leaf, ch 2, dc in same st, ch 2, sl st in same st, sl st in each of next 2 chs] twice.

2ND LEAF
Ch 9, dc in 2nd ch from hook, ch 2, sl st in same ch, ch 4, dc in 2nd ch from hook, ch 2, sl st in

same ch, ch 3, 3 dc in 2nd ch from hook, ch 2, sl st in same ch, sl st in next ch, [sl st in base of nob of leaf, ch 2, dc in same st, ch 2, sl st in same st, sl st in each of next 2 chs] twice.

3RD & 4TH LEAVES
[Ch 9, dc in 2nd ch from hook, ch 2, sl st in same ch, ch 3, 3 dc in 2nd ch from hook, ch 2, sl st in same ch, sl st in next ch, sl st in base of nob of leaf, ch 2, dc in same st, ch 2, sl st in same st, sl st in each of next 2 chs] twice.

TOP OF FERN
Ch 4, dc in 2nd ch from hook, ch 2, sl st in same ch, ch 3, 3 dc in 2nd ch from hook, ch 2, sl st in same ch, sl st in next ch, sl st in base of nob of leaf, ch 2, dc in same st, ch 2, sl st in same st, sl st in each of next 2 chs.

5TH & 6TH LEAVES
[Sl st in same ch as next leaf, ch 4, dc in 2nd ch from hook, ch 2, sl st in same ch, ch 3, 3 dc in 2nd ch from hook, ch 2, sl st in same ch, sl st in next ch, sl st in base of nob of leaf, ch 2, dc in same st, ch 2, sl st in same st, sl st in each of next 2 chs, sl st in each of next 4 chs in stem] twice.

7TH LEAF
Sl st in same ch as next leaf, ch 4, dc in 2nd ch from hook, ch 2, sl st in same ch, ch 4, dc in 2nd ch from hook, ch 2, sl st in same ch, ch 3, 3 dc in 2nd ch from hook, ch 2, sl st in same ch, sl st in next ch, [sl st in base of nob of leaf, ch 2, dc in same st, ch 2, sl st in same st, sl st in next 2 chs] twice, sl st in each of next 4 chs in stem.

8TH LEAF & STEM
Sl st in same ch as next leaf, ch 4, dc in 2nd ch from hook, ch 2, sl st in same ch, ch 4, dc in 2nd ch from hook, ch 2, sl st in same ch, ch 3, 3 dc in 2nd ch from hook, ch 2, sl st in same ch, sl st in next ch, [sl st in base of nob of leaf, ch 2, dc in same st, ch 2, sl st in same st, sl st in each of next 2 ch sts] twice, sl st in each of next 6 chs in stem. Fasten off. Weave in ends.

14B. FERN

SKILL LEVEL

INTERMEDIATE

FINISHED MEASUREMENTS

2½ inches wide x 4 inches long

MATERIALS

- Size 10 crochet cotton:
  25 yds white
- Size 7/1.65mm steel crochet hook

FIRST LEAF & STEM

Ch 15, dc in 2nd ch from hook, ch 2, sl st in same ch *(leaf nob made)*, ch 4, dc in 2nd ch from hook, ch 2, sl st in same ch, ch 3, 3 dc in 2nd ch from hook, ch 2, sl st in same ch, 2 sc over next ch, [sl st in base of nob of leaf, ch 2, dc in same st, ch 2, sl st in same st, 3 sc over next 2 chs] twice.

2ND LEAF

Ch 10, dc in 2nd ch from hook, ch 2, sl st in same ch, ch 4, dc in 2nd ch from hook, ch 2, sl st in same ch, ch 3, 3 dc in 2nd ch from hook, ch 2, sl st in same ch, 2 sc over next ch, [sl st in base of nob of leaf, ch 2, dc in same st, ch 2, sl st in same st, 3 sc over next 2 chs] twice.

3RD & 4TH LEAVES

[Ch 10, dc in 2nd ch from hook, ch 2, sl st in same ch, ch 3, 3 dc in 2nd ch from hook, ch 2, sl st in same ch, 2 sc over next ch, sl st in base of nob of leaf, ch 2, dc in same st, ch 2, sl st in same st, 3 sc over next 2 chs] twice.

TOP OF FERN

Ch 4, dc in 2nd ch from hook, ch 2, sl st in same ch, ch 3, 3 dc in 2nd ch from hook, ch 2, sl st in same ch, 2 sc over next ch, sl st in base of nob of leaf, ch 2, dc in same st, ch 2, sl st in same st, 3 sc over next 2 chs.

5TH & 6TH LEAVES

[Sl st in base of next leaf, ch 4, dc in 2nd ch from hook, ch 2, sl st in same ch, ch 3, 3 dc in 2nd ch from hook, ch 2, sl st in same ch, 2 sc over next ch, sl st in base of nob on leaf, ch 2, dc in same st, ch 2, sl st in same st, 3 sc over next 2 ch sts, 5 sc over in next 4 ch sts on stem] twice.

7TH LEAF

Sl st in base of next leaf, ch 4, dc in 2nd ch from hook, ch 2, sl st in same ch, ch 4, dc in 2nd ch from hook, ch 2, sl st in same ch, ch 3, 3 dc in 2nd ch from hook, ch 2, sl st in same ch, 2 sc over next ch, [sl st in base of nob on leaf, ch 2, dc in same st, ch 2, sl st in same st, 3 sc over next 2 chs] twice, sl st in each of next 4 ch sts in stem.

8TH LEAF & STEM

Sl st in base of next leaf, ch 4, dc in 2nd ch from hook, ch 2, sl st in same ch, ch 4, dc in 2nd ch from hook, ch 2, sl st in same ch, ch 3, 3 dc in 2nd ch from hook, ch 2, sl st in same ch, 2 sc over next ch, [sl st in base of nob on leaf, ch 2, dc in same st, ch 2, sl st in same st, 3 sc over next 2 chs] twice, 14 sc over rem ch sts of stem, sl st in next first ch st of stem. Fasten off. Weave in ends. ∎

Chapter 4 FILL-IN MOTIFS

Fill-in motifs are used to fill in spaces of your design. They are done in a variety of shapes to fit those spaces and add interest.

1. THREE RINGS WITH PICOTS PR

SKILL LEVEL

INTERMEDIATE

FINISHED MEASUREMENTS
1¾ inches wide x
1⅛ inches long

MATERIALS
- Size 10 crochet cotton: 10 yds white
- Size 7/1.65mm steel crochet hook
- Size G/6/4mm crochet hook for pc

Cut enough white thread for 4 12-wrap pc rings; set aside.

BASE RING & RING 1
Using nonworking end of a size G hook, with white, make a 12-wrap pc ring, 4 sc in ring, ch 2, using the nonworking end of a size G hook, make a 12-wrap pc ring with white, 3 sc in new ring, ch-3 picot in last sc made, [2 sc in same ring, ch-3 picot in last sc made] 4 times, 3 sc in same ring, sl st in first sc on ring, 3 sc over ch-2, 3 sc in first ring.

RINGS 2 & 3
[Ch 2, using the nonworking end of a size G hook, with white, make a 12-wrap pc ring, 3 sc in new ring, ch 1, sl st in last picot made on previous ring, ch 1, sl st in last sc made, (2 sc in same ring, ch-3 picot in last sc made) 4 times, 3 sc in same ring, sl st in first sc on ring, 3 sc over ch-2, 3 sc in first ring] twice, ending with sl st in first sc. Fasten off. Weave in ends.

2. FAN PC & PR

SKILL LEVEL

INTERMEDIATE

FINISHED MEASUREMENTS
2½ inches wide x
2 inches long

MATERIALS
- Size 10 crochet cotton: 15 yds white
- Size 7/1.65mm steel crochet hook
- Size G/6/4mm crochet hook for pc

Cut enough white thread for 6 12-wrap pc rings; set aside.

Padding cord lengths: Cut 2 lengths of white thread each 12 inches long for padding cord, hold tog and fold in half.

Rnd 1: Using the nonworking end of a size G hook, with white, make a 12-wrap pc ring, 16 sc in ring, join in first sc.

Row 1: Now working in rows, ch 4 *(counts as first tr, ch 1)*, tr in next sc, [ch 1, tr in next sc] 7 times, turn.

Row 2: Ch 1, sc in next ch-1 sp and through fold of padding cord, work over all 4 strands of padding cord across, 2 sc in same sp, [2 sc in next ch-1 sp] 6 times, 3 sc in next ch-1 sp, turn.

Row 3: Ch 1, working over padding cord across, sc in each sc across, drop padding cord, turn.

Row 4: Ch 4, sk next 2 sc, sc in next sc, [ch 4, sk next 2 sc, sc in next sc] 5 times, turn.

Row 5: Ch 1, 3 sc in next ch-4 sp, ch 2, using nonworking end of a size G hook, make a 12-wrap pc ring, 12 sc in ring, 2 sc over ch-2,

3 sc in same ch-4 sp, [3 sc in next ch-4 sp, ch 2, using the nonworking end of a size G hook, make a 12-wrap pc ring, 3 sc in ring, sl st in 9th sc on previous ring, 9 sc in ring, 2 sc over ch-2, 3 sc in same ch 4 sp] 4 times. Fasten off. Weave in ends.

3. 12 GRAPE CLUSTER PC & PR

SKILL LEVEL

INTERMEDIATE

FINISHED MEASUREMENTS
2 inches wide x 2½ inches long

MATERIALS

- Size 10 crochet cotton: 30 yds white
- Size 7/1.65mm steel crochet hook

Cut enough white thread for 12 pc rings; set aside.

Padding cord lengths: Cut 2 lengths of white thread each 7 inches long for padding cord, hold tog and fold in half.

GRAPE 1
Using the nonworking end of a size G hook throughout and with white, make a 12-wrap pc ring, 16 sc in ring, join in first sc. Fasten off. Weave in end.

GRAPE 2
Make a 12-wrap pc ring, 15 sc in ring, sl st in any sc on Grape 1, sc in ring, join in first sc. Fasten off. Weave in end.

GRAPE 3
Make a 12-wrap pc ring, 11 sc in ring, sl st in the 4th sc before the previous ring joining on Grape 1, 4 sc in ring, sl st in 4th sc from ring joining on the Grape 2, sc in ring, join in first sc. Fasten off. Weave in end.

GRAPE 4
Make a 12-wrap pc ring, 15 sc in ring, sl st over the joining between Grape 2 and Grape 3, sc in ring, join in first sc. Fasten off. Weave in end.

GRAPE 5
Make a 12-wrap pc ring, 11 sc in ring, sl st in the 4th sc before previous ring joining on Grape 3, 4 sc in ring, sl st in the 4th sc from ring joining on the Grape 4, sc in ring, join in first sc. Fasten off. Weave in end.

GRAPE 6
Make a 12-wrap pc ring, 11 sc in ring, sl st in the 4th sc before the ring joining on Grape 4, 4 sc in ring, sl st in the 4th sc from ring joining on Grape 2, sc in ring, join in first sc. Fasten off. Weave in end.

GRAPE 7
Make a 12-wrap pc ring, 15 sc in ring, sl st over the joining between Grape 4 and Grape 6, sc in ring, join in first sc. Fasten off. Weave in end.

GRAPE 8
Make a 12-wrap pc ring, 11 sc in ring, sl st over the joining between Grape 5 and Grape 4, 4 sc in ring, sl st in the 4th sc from ring joining on Grape 7, sc in ring, join in first sc. Fasten off. Weave in end.

GRAPE 9
Make a 12-wrap pc ring, 11 sc in ring, sl st in the 4th sc before the previous ring joining on Grape 5, 4 sc in ring, sl st in the 4th sc from ring joining on Grape 8, sc in ring, join in first sc. Fasten off. Weave in end.

GRAPE 10
Make a 12-wrap pc ring, 11 sc in ring, sl st in the 4th sc before the ring joining on Grape 7, 4 sc in ring, sl st in the 4th sc from ring joining on the Grape 6, sc in ring, join in first sc. Fasten off. Weave in end.

GRAPE 11
Make a 12-wrap pc ring, 9 sc in ring, sl st in 3rd sc on Grape 9 from the joining between Grapes 8 and 9 that will have you working toward the joining, 3 sc in ring, sl st over the joining between Grape 8 and Grape 9, 3 sc in ring, sk

next 2 sc on Grape 8, sl st in next sc, sc in ring, join in first sc. Fasten off. Weave in end.

GRAPE 12
Make a 12-wrap pc ring, 9 sc in ring, sl st in the 3rd sc on Grape 7 from the joining between Grapes 7 and 10 that will have you working toward the joining, 3 sc in ring, sl st over the joining between Grapes 7 and 10, 3 sc in ring, sk next 2 sc on Grape 10, sl st in next sc, sc in ring, join in first sc. Fasten off. Weave in end.

STEM
Join thread in joining between rings 7 and 8, ch 16, turn, sc in 2nd ch and through the fold of padding cord threads, work over all 4 strands of the padding cord threads on Stem, sc in each of next 14 sc, sl st in ring joining, adjust padding cord. Fasten off. Weave in end.

4. RING MOTIF: TRADITIONAL PR

SKILL LEVEL

EXPERIENCED

FINISHED MEASUREMENT
2 inches across

MATERIALS
- Size 10 crochet cotton: 25 yds white
- Size 7/1.65mm steel crochet hook
- Size K/10½/6.5mm crochet hook for pc
- Size H/8/5mm crochet hook

Cut enough white thread for 9 pc rings; set aside.

BASE RING & FIRST RING
Using the nonworking end of a size K hook and white, make a 12-wrap pc ring, 3 sc in ring, ch 2, using the nonworking end of size H hook make a 12-wrap pc ring, 4 sc in ring, [ch 3, 4 sc in ring] 3 times, 3 sc over ch 2.

RINGS 2–7
(3 sc in original ring, ch 2, using the nonworking end of a size H hook, make a 12-wrap pc ring,

4 sc in ring, ch 1, sc in last ch-3 sp on previous ring made, ch 1, 4 sc in ring, {ch 3, 4 sc in ring} twice, 3 sc over ch 2) 6 times.

RING 8
3 sc in original ring, ch 2, using nonworking end of a size H hook, make a 12-wrap pc ring, 4 sc in ring, ch 1, sc in last ch-3 sp on previous ring made, ch 1, 4 sc in ring, ch 3, 4 sc in ring, ch 1, sc in first ch-3 sp on first ring on circle, ch 1, 4 sc in ring, 3 sc over ch-2, join in first sc on original ring. Fasten off. Weave in end.

5A. SHAMROCK: TRADITIONAL WITH PC & PR

SKILL LEVEL

INTERMEDIATE

FINISHED MEASUREMENT
2½ inches across

MATERIALS
- Size 10 crochet cotton: 20 yds white
- Size 7/1.65mm steel crochet hook
- Size H/8/5mm crochet hook for pc

Padding cord lengths: With white, cut 2 lengths of thread 3 feet long for padding cord, hold tog and fold in half, wrap on padding cord bobbin.

Rnd 1: Using the nonworking end of size H hook and white, make a 12-wrap pc ring, [8 sc in ring, ch-3 picot in last sc made] 3 times, join in first sc.

Rnd 2: Sl st in next sc, ch 1, sc in same sc, sc in each of next 4 sc, ch 10, sk next 3 sc, [sc in each of next 5 sc, ch 10, sk next 3 sc] twice, join in first sc.

Rnd 3: Sl st in next sc, ch 1, sc in same sc, sc in each of next 2 sc, *ch 1, (sc in ch-10 lp, ch 1, hdc, ch 1, dc, {ch 2, tr} 4 times, ch 2, dc, ch 1, hdc, ch 1, sc) in same ch-10 lp, ch 1**, sk next sc, sc in each of next 3 sc, rep from * around, ending last rep at **, join in first sc.

Rnd 4: Ch 1, sc in same sc and through the fold of padding cord threads, work over all 4 strands of padding cord threads around, sc in next sc, ch-3 picot in last sc made, sc in same sc, sc in next sc, sc in 2nd ch-1 sp on petal, sc in next ch-1 sp, ch-3 picot in last sc made, sc in same sp, [2 sc in next ch-2 sp, ch-3 picot in last sc made, sc in same sp] 5 times, sc in next ch-1 sp, ch-3 picot in last sc made, sc in same sp, sc in next ch-1 sp, sk next ch-1 sp, sc in next sc, {sc in next sc, ch-3 picot in last sc made, sc in same sc, sc in next sc, sc in 2nd ch-1 sp on petal, sc in next ch-1 sp, ch-3 picot in last sc made, sc in same sp, [2 sc in next ch-2 sp, ch-3 picot in last sc made, sc in same sp] 5 times, sc in next ch-1 sp, ch-3 picot in last sc made, sc in same sp, sc in next ch-1 sp, sk next ch-1 sp, sc in next sc} twice, join in first sc. Fasten off. Weave in end.

5B. SHAMROCK: UPDATED

SKILL LEVEL

INTERMEDIATE

FINISHED MEASUREMENT
2½ inches across

MATERIALS
• Size 10 crochet cotton: 20 yds white
• Size 7/1.65mm steel crochet hook

Rnd 1: Ch 6, sl st to form ring, ch 1, [8 sc in ring, ch-3 picot in last sc made] 3 times, join in first sc.

Rnd 2: Sl st in next sc, ch 1, sc in same sc, sc in each of next 4 sc, ch 10, sk next 3 sc, [sc in each of next 5 sc, ch 10, sk next 3 sc] twice, join in first sc.

Rnd 3: Sl st in next sc, ch 1, sc in same st, sc in each of next 2 sc, ch 1, (sc, ch 1, hdc, ch 1, dc, {ch 2, tr} 4 times, ch 2, dc, ch 1, hdc, ch 1, sc) in next ch-10 lp, ch 1, [sc in each of next 3 sc, ch

1, (sc, ch 1, hdc, ch 1, dc, {ch 2, tr} 4 times, ch 2, dc, ch 1, hdc, ch 1, sc) in next ch-10 lp, ch 1] twice, join in first sc.

Rnd 4: Ch 1, sc in same sc, sc in next sc, ch-3 picot in last sc made, sc in same sc, ch 1, sc in 2nd ch-1 sp on petal, sc in next ch-1 sp, ch-3 picot in last sc made, sc in same sp, (2 sc in next ch-2 sp, ch-3 picot in last sc made, sc in same sp) 5 times, sc in next ch-1 sp, ch-3 picot in last sc made, sc in same sp, sc in next ch-1 sp, sk next ch-1 sp, [sc in each of next 2 sc, ch-3 picot in last sc made, sc in same sc, sc in next sc, sc in 2nd ch-1 sp on petal, sc in next ch-1 sp, ch-3 picot in last sc made, sc in same sp, (2 sc in next ch-2 sp, ch-3 picot in last sc made, sc in same sp) 5 times, sc in next ch-1 sp, ch-3 picot in last sc made, sc in same sp, sc in next ch-1 sp, sk next ch-1 sp] twice, join in first sc. Fasten off. Weave in end.

6A. PINWHEEL: TRADITIONAL PC & PR

SKILL LEVEL
INTERMEDIATE

FINISHED MEASUREMENT
2½ inches across

MATERIALS
• Size 10 crochet cotton: 25 yds white
• Size 7/1.65mm steel crochet hook
• Size G/6/4mm crochet hook for pc

Note: *This is a one-way design. Motif will swirl in one direction for a right-handed person and in the opposite direction for a left-handed person.*

Padding cord lengths: Cut 2 lengths of white thread each 5 feet long for padding cord, hold tog and fold in half, wrap on padding cord bobbin.

Rnd 1: Using nonworking end of size G hook, make 12-wrap pc ring, 12 sc in ring, join in first sc.

Rnd 2 (Petal 1): Ch 1, sc in same sc and through the fold of padding cord threads, 20 sc worked over all 4 strands of padding cord only, adjust padding cord at this point, turn, working over all 4 strands of padding cord, sc in each of next 2 sc, ch-3 picot in last sc made, [sc in each of next 4 sc, ch-3 picot in last sc made] 4 times, sc in each of last 2 sc on petal, adjust padding cord, sc in each of next 2 sc on ring.

Petals 2–5: Turn, with RS facing, 20 sc over padding cord only, without turning, sl st in 2nd picot from the ring on previous petal, adjust padding cord, turn, with WS facing, working over all 4 strands of padding cord, sc in each of next 2 sc, ch-3 picot in last sc made, [sc in each of next 4 sc, ch-3 picot in last sc made] 4 times, sc in each of last 2 sc on petal, adjust padding cord, sc in each of next 2 sc on ring.

Petal 6: Turn, with RS facing, 20 sc over padding cord only, without turning, sl st in 2nd picot from the ring on previous petal, adjust padding cord, turn, with WS facing, working over all 4 strands of padding cord, sc in each of next 2 sc, ch-3 picot in last sc made, [sc in each of next 4 sc, ch-3 picot in last sc made] twice, sc in each of next 4 sc, ch 1, sl st in tip of first petal, ch 1, sl st in last sc made, sc in each of next 4 sc, ch-3 picot in last sc made, sc in each of last 2 sc on petal, sc in next sc on ring, join in first sc. Fasten off. Weave in ends.

6B. PINWHEEL: UPDATED

SKILL LEVEL

INTERMEDIATE

FINISHED MEASUREMENT
3 inches across

MATERIALS

- Size 10 crochet cotton:
  20 yds white
- Size 7/1.65mm steel crochet hook

Note: *This is a one-way design. Motif will swirl in one direction for a right-handed person and in the opposite direction for a left-handed person.*

Rnd 1: Ch 5, sl st to form ring, 12 sc in ring, join in first sc.

Rnd 2: Petal 1: Ch 17, turn, sc in 2nd ch from hook, hdc in next ch, ch-3 picot in last hdc made, [dc in next ch, 2 dc in next ch, dc in next ch, ch-3 picot in last dc made] 4 times, hdc in each of last 2 chs, sc in each of next 2 sc on ring.

Petals 2–5: Ch 16, sl st in 2nd picot from ring on previous petal, turn, sc in next ch st, hdc in next ch st, ch-3 picot in last hdc made, [dc in next ch, 2 dc in next ch, dc in next ch, ch-3 picot in last dc made] 4 times, hdc in each of last 2 chs, sc in each of next 2 sc on ring.

Petal 6: Ch 16, sl st in 2nd picot from ring on previous petal, turn, sc in next ch, hdc in next ch, ch-3 picot in last hdc made, [dc in next ch, 2 dc in next ch, dc in next ch, ch-3 picot in last dc made] twice, dc in next ch, 2 dc in next ch, dc in next ch, ch 1, sl st in tip of first petal, ch 1, sl st in last dc made, dc in next ch, 2 dc in next ch, dc in next ch, ch-3 picot in last dc made, hdc in each of last 2 chs, sc in next sc on ring, join in first sc. Fasten off. Weave in ends.

7A. 6-POINT MOTIF TRADITIONAL PC & PR

SKILL LEVEL

INTERMEDIATE

FINISHED MEASUREMENT
3⅛ inches across

MATERIALS

- Size 10 crochet cotton:
  12 yds white
- Size 7/1.65mm steel crochet hook
- Size G/6/4mm crochet hook for pc

Padding cord lengths: Cut 2 lengths of white thread each 5 feet long for padding cord, hold tog and fold in half, wrap on padding cord bobbin.

Rnd 1: Using nonworking end of size G hook, make 12-wrap pc ring, 18 sc in ring, join in first sc.

Rnd 2: Ch 1, sc in same sc, ch 14, dc in the 9th ch from hook, ch 2, sk next 2 chs, dc in next ch, ch 2, sk 1 sc on ring, [sc in each of next 2 sc, ch 14, dc in 9th ch from hook, ch 2, sk next 2 chs, dc in next ch, ch 2, sk 1 sc on ring] 5 times, ending with sc in next sc, join in first sc. Fasten off. Weave in ends.

Rnd 3: Join thread in ch-8 sp on tip of any point, ch 1, sc in same sp and through the fold of padding cord, work over all 4 strands of padding cord around, sc in same sp, [ch 2, 2 sc in same sp] 5 times, 2 sc in next ch-2 sp, ch 2, 2 sc in same sp, [3 sc in next ch-2 sp] twice, 2 sc in next ch-2 sp, ch 2, turn, (sc, sl st, turn) in last ch-2 sp on previous point, (sc, ch 3, sc) in ch-2 sp between points, ch 2, 2 sc in ch-2 sp on working point, [2 sc in next ch-8 sp, (ch 2, 2 sc in same ch-8 sp) 5 times, (2 sc, ch 2, 2 sc) in next ch-2 sp, (3 sc in next ch-2 sp) twice, 2 sc in next ch-2 sp, ch 2, turn, (sc, sl st, turn) in last ch-2 sp on previous point, (sc, ch 3, sc) in ch-2 sp between points, ch 2, 2 sc in ch-2 sp on working point] around, join in first sc. Fasten off. Weave in ends.

7B. 6-POINT MOTIF: UPDATED

SKILL LEVEL

INTERMEDIATE

FINISHED MEASUREMENT
3¼ inches across

MATERIALS
- Size 10 crochet cotton:
  12 yds white
- Size 7/1.65mm steel crochet hook

Rnd 1: Ch 5, sl st to form ring, ch 1, 18 sc in ring, join in first sc.

Rnd 2: Ch 1, sc in same sc, ch 14, dc in the 9th ch from hook, ch 2, sk next 2 chs, dc in next ch, ch 2, sk 1 sc on ring, [sc in each of next 2 sc, ch 14, dc in the 9th ch from hook, ch 2, sk next 2 chs, dc in next ch, ch 2, sk 1 sc on ring] 5 times, ending with sc in next sc, join in first sc. Fasten off. Weave in ends.

Rnd 3: Join thread in ch-8 sp on tip of any point, ch 1, 2 sc in same sp, [ch 2, 2 sc in same sp] 5 times, 2 sc in next ch-2 sp, ch 2, 2 sc in same sp, [3 sc in next ch-2 sp] twice, 2 sc in next ch-2 sp, ch 2, turn, (sc, sl st, turn) in last ch-2 sp on previous point, (sc, ch 3, sc) in ch-2 sp between points, ch 2, 2 sc in ch-2 sp on working point, [2 sc in next ch-8 sp, (ch 2, 2 sc in same ch-8 sp) 5 times, (2 sc, ch 2, 2 sc) in next ch-2 sp, (3 sc in next ch-2 sp) twice, 2 sc in next ch-2 sp, ch 2, turn, (sc, sl st, turn) in last ch-2 sp on previous point, (sc, ch 3, sc) in ch-2 sp between points, ch 2, 2 sc in ch-2 sp on working point] around, join in first sc. Fasten off. Weave in ends.

8A. 3-POINT MOTIF: TRADITIONAL PC & PR

SKILL LEVEL

INTERMEDIATE

FINISHED MEASUREMENT
3½ inches at widest point

MATERIALS
- Size 10 crochet cotton:
  15 yds white
- Size 7/1.65mm steel crochet hook
- Size G/6/4mm crochet hook for pc

Padding cord lengths: Cut 2 lengths of white thread each 4 feet long for padding cord, hold tog and fold in half, wrap on padding cord bobbin.

Rnd 1: Using nonworking end of size G hook, make 12-wrap pc ring, 18 sc in ring, join in first sc.

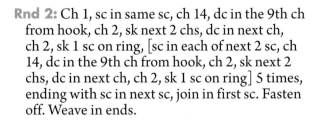

Point 1: Ch 2, dc in each of next 5 sc, turn, sl st in 2nd dc, ch 2, dc in each of next 3 dc, turn, sl st in 2nd dc, ch 2, dc in next dc, turn, sl st in sp between 2 dc, ch 6, sl st in 6th ch from hook to form ring, ch 1, 10 sc in ring just formed, sl st around base of ring, turn, sc in next sc, [ch 4, sc in each of next 2 sc] 4 times, ch 4, sc in next sc, join in base of ring. Fasten off. Weave in ends.

Points 2 & 3: With RS facing, join thread in next sc on ring, follow instructions for first point.

Rnd 2: Join thread between any 2 points and through the fold of the padding cord, work over all 4 strands of padding cord around, {3 sc over post of dc of first row of point, [3 sc over post of dc of next row] twice, sl st around base of ring at top of point, sl st in next sc, [7 sc in next ch-4 sp, sl st between next 2 sc] 4 times, 7 sc in next ch-4 sp, sl st in next sc, sl st around base of ring, [3 sc over post of next dc] 3 times, sl st between points} 3 times. Fasten off. Weave in ends.

8B. 3-POINT MOTIF: UPDATED

SKILL LEVEL

INTERMEDIATE

FINISHED MEASUREMENT
3⅝ inches at widest point

MATERIALS
- Size 10 crochet cotton:
  15 yds white
- Size 7/1.65mm steel crochet hook

Rnd 1: With white ch 5, sl st to form ring, ch 1, 18 sc in ring, join in first sc.

Point 1: Ch 2, dc in each of next 5 sc, turn, sl st in 2nd dc, ch 2, dc in each of next 3 dc, turn, sl st in 2nd dc, ch 2, dc in next dc, turn, sl st between 2 dc, ch 6, sl st in 6th ch from hook to form ring, ch 1, 10 sc in ring just formed, sl st around base of ring, turn, sc in next sc, [ch 4, sc in each

of next 2 sc] 4 times, ch 4, sc in next sc, join in base of ring. Fasten off. Weave in ends.

Points 2 & 3: With RS facing, join thread in next sc on ring, follow instructions for first point.

Rnd 2 (RS): Join thread between any 2 points {3 sc over post of dc of first row of point, [3 sc over post of dc of next row] twice, sl st around base of ring at top of point, sl st in next sc, [7 sc in next ch-4 sp, sl st between next 2 sc] 4 times, 7 sc in next ch-4 sp, sl st in next sc, sl st around base of ring, [3 sc over post of next dc] 3 times, sl st between points} 3 times. Fasten off. Weave in ends.

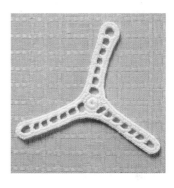

9A. 3-SPOKE WHEEL: TRADITIONAL PC & PR

SKILL LEVEL

INTERMEDIATE

FINISHED MEASUREMENT
4¼ inches at widest point

MATERIALS
- Size 10 crochet cotton:
  10 yds white
  Size 7/1.65mm steel crochet hook
  Size G/6/4mm crochet hook for pc

Padding cord lengths: Cut 2 lengths of white thread each 4 feet long for padding cord, hold tog and fold in half, wrap on padding cord bobbin.

Rnd 1: Using nonworking end of size G hook, make 12-wrap pc ring, 15 sc in ring, join in first sc.

Rnd 2: Ch 1, sc in same sc, {ch 26, dc in 9th ch from hook, [ch 2, sk next 2 chs, dc in next ch] 5 times, ch 2, sk next sc on ring, sc in each of next 4 sc} twice, ch 26, dc in 9th ch from hook, [ch 2, sk next 2 chs, dc in next ch] 5 times, ch 2, sk next sc on ring, sc in each of next 3 sc, join in first sc.

Rnd 3: Sl st through fold of padding cord, {[3 sc in next ch-2 sp] 6 times, 12 sc in next ch-8 sp, [3 sc in next ch-2 sp] 6 times, sk next sc, sc in each of next 2 sc} 3 times, join in first sc. Fasten off. Weave in ends.

9B. 3-SPOKE WHEEL: UPDATED

SKILL LEVEL

INTERMEDIATE

FINISHED MEASUREMENT

4½ inches at widest point

MATERIALS

- Size 10 crochet cotton: 10 yds white
- Size 7/1.65mm steel crochet hook

Rnd 1: Ch 4, sl st to form ring, ch 1, 15 sc in ring, sl st in first sc.

Rnd 2: Ch 1, sc in same sc, {ch 26, dc in 9th ch from hook, [ch 2, sk next 2 chs, dc in next ch] 5 times, ch 2, sk next sc on ring, sc in each of next 4 sc} twice, ch 26, dc in 9th ch from hook, [ch 2, sk next 2 chs, dc in next ch] 5 times, ch 2, sk next sc on ring, sc in each of next 3 sc, join in first sc.

Rnd 3: {[3 sc in next ch-2 sp] 6 times, 12 sc in next ch-8 sp, [3 sc in next ch-2 sp] 6 times, sk next sc, sc in each of next 2 sc} 3 times, join in first sc. Fasten off. Weave in ends.

10. BULLION STITCH SCROLL

SKILL LEVEL

INTERMEDIATE

FINISHED MEASUREMENT

2½ inches wide x 1¾ inches long

MATERIALS

- Size 10 crochet cotton: 15 yds white
- Size 7/1.65mm steel crochet hook

Row 1: Ch 17, sc in 2nd ch from hook, sc in each of next 11 chs, [2 sc in next ch, sc in next ch] twice, sl st in the back lp of ch in the 8th ch from hook, turn.

Row 2: Ch 1, sc in next sc, dc in next sc, 7-wrap bullion st in next sc, ch 1, 8-wrap bullion st in next sc, ch 1, [9-wrap bullion st in next sc, ch 1, 9-wrap bullion st in same sc, ch 1] 3 times, 8-wrap bullion st in next sc, ch 1, 7-wrap bullion st in next sc, 6-wrap bullion st in next sc, 5-wrap bullion st in next sc, 4-wrap bullion st in next sc, dc in next sc, hdc in each of next 2 sc, sc in each of next 3 sc, (sc, sl st) in last sc, turn.

Row 3: Ch 1, sc in each of next 4 sc, sc in each of next 2 hdc, sc in next dc, sc in next 4-wrap bullion st, sc in next 5-wrap bullion st, sc in next 6-wrap bullion st, ch-3 picot in last sc made, sc in next 7-wrap bullion st, sc in next ch-1 sp, sc in next 8-wrap bullion st, ch-3 picot in last sc made, [sc in next ch-1 sp, sc in next 9-wrap bullion st, ch-3 picot in last sc made] 6 times, sc in next ch-1 sp, sc in next 8-wrap bullion st, ch-3 picot in last sc made, sc in next ch-1 sp, sc in next 7-wrap bullion st, ch-3 picot in last sc made, sc in next dc, sc in next sc, join in joining at end of row 1. Fasten off. Weave in ends.

46

11A. SCROLL: TRADITIONAL PC

SKILL LEVEL
INTERMEDIATE

FINISHED MEASUREMENT
3⅛ inches wide x 1⅞ inches long

MATERIALS
- Size 10 crochet cotton: 25 yds white
- Size 7/1.65mm steel crochet hook

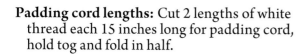

Padding cord lengths: Cut 2 lengths of white thread each 15 inches long for padding cord, hold tog and fold in half.

Row 1: Ch 25, sc in 2nd ch from hook, sc in each of next 17 chs, [2 sc in next ch, sc in next ch] 3 times, sl st in back lp of ch in 8th ch from hook, turn.

Row 2: Ch 1, sc in first sc, ch 1, hdc in next sc, [ch 2, dc in next sc] 6 times, [ch 1, sk next sc, dc in next sc] 6 times, [ch 1, sk next sc, hdc in next sc] twice, ch 1, sk next sc, sc in next sc, 2 sc in last sc, turn.

Row 3: Ch 1, sc in first sc and through fold of padding cord threads, work over all 4 strands of padding cord threads across, sc in each of next 2 sc, sc in next ch-1 sp, ch-3 picot in last sc made, sc in same sp, {[2 sc in next ch-1 sp] twice, ch 5, turn, sk next 3 sc, sc in next sc, sl st in next sc, ch 1, turn, 3 sc in ch-5 sp, ch-3 picot in last sc made, 5 sc in same sp, ch-3 picot in last sc made, 2 sc in same sp, sc in same ch-1 sp on scroll} 3 times, [2 sc in next ch-1 sp] twice, 2 sc in next ch-2 sp, ch 5, turn, sk next 3 sc, sc in next sc, sl st in next sc, ch 1, turn, 3 sc in ch-5 sp, ch-3 picot in last sc made, 5 sc in same sp, ch-3 picot in last sc made, 2 sc in same sp, sc in same ch-2 sp on scroll, 4 sc

in next ch-2 sp, 2 sc in next ch-2 sp, ch 5, turn, sk next 3 sc, sc in next sc, sl st in next sc, ch 1, turn, 3 sc in ch-5 sp, ch-3 picot in last sc made, 5 sc in same sp, ch-3 picot in last sc made, 2 sc in same sp, sc in same ch-2 sp on scroll, 2 sc in next ch-1 sp, sc in next sc, ch 3, turn, sk next sc, sc in next sc, sl st in next sc, ch 1, turn, 2 sc in ch-3 sp, ch-3 picot in last sc made, 3 sc in same sp, ch-3 picot in last sc made, sc in same sp, sc in same sc, sl st in joining at end of row 1. Fasten off. Weave in ends.

11B. SCROLL: UPDATED

SKILL LEVEL
INTERMEDIATE

FINISHED MEASUREMENT
3⅛ inches wide x 2 inches long

MATERIALS
- Size 10 crochet cotton: 25 yds white
- Size 7/1.65mm steel crochet hook

Row 1: Ch 25, sc in 2nd ch from hook, sc in each of next 17 chs, [2 sc in next ch st, sc in next ch] 3 times, sl st in back lp of ch in the 8th ch from hook, turn.

Row 2: Ch 1, sc in first sc, ch 1, hdc in next sc, [ch 2, dc in next sc] 6 times, [ch 1, sk next sc, dc in next sc] 6 times, [ch 1, sk next sc, hdc in next sc] twice, ch 1, sk next sc, sc in each of next 2 sc, sc in same sc, turn.

Row 3: Ch 1, sc in first sc, sc in each of next 2 sc, sc in next ch-1 sp, ch-3 picot in last sc made, sc in same sp, {[2 sc in next ch-1 sp] twice, ch 5, turn, sk next 3 sc, sc in next sc, sl st in next sc, ch 1, turn, 3 sc in ch-5 sp, ch-3 picot in last sc made, 5 sc in same sp, ch-3 picot in last sc made, 2 sc in same sp, sc in same ch-1 sp on scroll} 3 times, [2 sc in next ch-1 sp] twice, 2 sc in next ch-2 sp, ch 5, turn, sk next 3 sc, sc in next sc, sl st in next sc, ch 1, turn, 3 sc in ch-5 sp, ch-3 picot in last sc made, 5 sc in same sp, ch-3 picot in last sc made, 2 sc in same sp, 3 sc in same ch-2 sp on scroll, 4 sc in next ch-2 sp, ch 5, turn, sk next 3 sc, sc in next sc, sl st in next sc, ch 1, turn, 3 sc in ch-5 sp, ch-3 picot in last sc made, 5 sc in same sp, ch-3 picot in last sc made, 2 sc in same sp, sc in same ch-2 sp on scroll, 4 sc in next ch-2 sp, 2 sc in next ch-2 sp, ch 5, turn, sk next 3 sc, sc in next sc, sl st in next sc, ch 1, turn, 3 sc in ch-5 sp, ch-3 picot in last sc made, 5 sc in same sp, ch-3 picot in last sc made, 2 sc in same sp, sc in same ch-2 sp on scroll, 2 sc in next ch-1 sp, sc in next sc, ch 3, turn, sk next sc, sc in next sc, sl st in next sc, ch 1, turn, 2 sc in ch-3 sp, ch-3 picot in last sc made, 3 sc in same sp, ch-3 picot in last sc made, sc in same sp, sc in same sc, sl st in joining at end of row 1. Fasten off. Weave in ends.

12A. SCROLL WITH PICOTS: TRADITIONAL PC

SKILL LEVEL

INTERMEDIATE

FINISHED MEASUREMENT
2⅞ inches wide x 1⅝ inches long

MATERIALS
- Size 10 crochet cotton:
  25 yds white
- Size 7/1.65mm steel crochet hook

Padding cord lengths: Cut 2 lengths of white thread each 15 inches long for padding cord, hold tog and fold in half.

Row 1: Ch 25, sc in 2nd ch from hook and through fold of padding cord threads, work over all 4 strands of padding cord threads across, sc in each of next 17 chs, [2 sc in next ch st, sc in next ch st] 3 times, sl st in back lp of the ch in 8th ch from hook, drop padding cord, turn.

Row 2: Ch 1, sc in first sc, [ch 3, sc in next sc] 6 times, [ch 3, sk next sc, sc in next sc] 9 times, ch 1, sk next sc, hdc in next sc, turn.

Row 3: Ch 1, sc in same sp, [ch 3, sc in next ch-3 sp] 15 times, ch 3, sc in next sc, sl st in joining at end of first row, turn.

Row 4: Ch 1, pick up padding cord, work over all 4 strands of padding cord threads across, [2 sc in next ch-3 sp, ch-3 picot in last sc made, 2 sc in same sp] 15 times, 4 sc in next ch-3 sp, 3 sc over post of hdc, sl st in first sc of row 1. Fasten off. Weave in ends.

12B. SCROLL WITH PICOTS: UPDATED

SKILL LEVEL

INTERMEDIATE

FINISHED MEASUREMENT
3 inches wide x 1¾ inches long

MATERIALS
- Size 10 crochet cotton:
  25 yds white
- Size 7/1.65mm steel crochet hook

Row 1: With white ch 25, sc in 2nd ch from hook, sc in each of next 17 chs, [2 sc in next ch, sc in next ch] 3 times, sl st in back lp of ch in 8th ch from hook, turn.

Row 2: Ch 1, sc in first sc, [ch 3, sc in next sc] 6 times, [ch 3, sk next sc, sc in next sc] 9 times, ch 1, sk next sc, hdc in next sc, turn.

Row 3: Ch 1, sc in first sp, [ch 3, sc in next ch-3 sp] 15 times, ch 3, sc in next sc, sl st in joining at end of first row.

Row 4: Ch 1, [2 sc in next ch-3 sp, ch-3 picot in last sc made, 2 sc in same sp] 15 times, 4 sc in next ch-3 sp, 3 sc over post of hdc, sl st in first sc of row 1. Fasten off. Weave in ends. ▪

Chapter 5 EDGINGS & INSERTIONS

There is nothing like a good edging to finish a piece. I have provided some basic Irish crochet edgings, from the very simple to the more complex. Insertions can be used on towels, runners, curtains, skirts and made even more special when a matching edging is used with it.

1. EDGING SINGLE PICOTS ACROSS

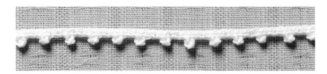

SKILL LEVEL

EASY

FINISHED MEASUREMENTS
Each rep [1 picot, 3 sc] = ⅜ inch wide x ¼ inch tall

MATERIALS
- Size 10 crochet cotton:
  White amount needed varies by length of edging
- Size 7/1.65mm steel crochet hook

Note: *Edging has multiple of 3 plus 1. Sample: 27 x 3 = 81 + 1 = 82 + 1 for turning ch = 83 total.*

Row 1: Ch 83, sc in 2nd ch from hook, ch 3 picot in last sc made, [sc in each of next 3 chs, ch 3 picot in last sc made] across. Fasten off. Weave in ends.

2. EDGING SIMPLE

SKILL LEVEL

EASY

FINISHED MEASUREMENTS
Each rep = 1 inch wide x ¾ inch tall

MATERIALS
- Size 10 crochet cotton:
  White amount needed varies by length of edging
- Size 7/1.65mm steel crochet hook

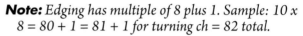

Note: *Edging has multiple of 8 plus 1. Sample: 10 x 8 = 80 + 1 = 81 + 1 for turning ch = 82 total.*

Row 1: Ch 82, sc in 2nd ch from hook, sc in each ch st across, turn. *(81 sts, 10 groups of 8 plus 1)*

Row 2: Ch 1, sc in first sc, sc in each of next 4 sc, ch 3 picot in last sc made, sc in each of next 3 sc, ch 8, turn, sk next 5 sc, sc in next sc, sl st in next sc, ch 1, turn, [3 sc in ch-8 sp, ch 3 picot in last sc made] 3 times, 2 sc in same sp, *sc in each of next 5 sc, ch 3 picot in last sc made, sc in each of next 3 sc, ch 8, turn, sk next 5 sc, sc in next sc, sl st in next sc, ch 1, turn, [3 sc in ch-8 sp, ch 3 picot in last sc made] 3 times, 2 sc in same sp, * rep from * to * across, join in next sc. Fasten off. Weave in ends.

3. EDGING ARCHES WITH PICOTS

SKILL LEVEL

INTERMEDIATE

FINISHED MEASUREMENTS
Each rep = 1¾ inches wide x 1 inch tall

MATERIALS
- Size 10 crochet cotton:
  White amount needed varies by length of edging
- Size 7/1.65mm steel crochet hook

Note: Edging has multiple of 15. Sample: 15 x 5 = 75 + 1 for turning ch = 76 total.

Row 1: Ch 76, sc in 2nd ch from hook, sc in each ch st across, turn.

Row 2: Ch 1, sc in first sc, sc in each of next 6 sc, ch 6, turn, sk next 4 sc, sc in next sc, sl st in next sc, ch 1, turn, 4 sc in ch-6 sp, ch 3 picot in last sc made, 6 sc in same sp, sc in each of next 7 sc, ch 6, turn, sk next 4 sc, sc in next sc, sl st in next sc, ch 1, turn, 4 sc in ch-6 sp, ch 7, turn, sc in 5th sc on previous arch, sl st in next sc, ch 1, turn, 4 sc in ch-7 sp, [ch 3 picot in last sc made, 4 sc in same sp] twice, 2 sc in ch-6 sp, ch 3 picot in last sc made, 4 sc in same sp, *sc in each of next 8 sc, ch 6, turn, sk next 4 sc, sc in next sc, sl st in next sc, ch 1, turn, 4 sc in ch-6 sp, ch 3 picot in last sc made, 6 sc in same sp, sc in each of next 7 sc, ch 6, turn, sk next 4 sc, sc in next sc, sl st in next sc, ch 1, turn, 4 sc in ch-6 sp, ch 7, turn, sc in 5th sc on previous arch, sl st in next sc, ch 1, turn, 4 sc in ch-7 sp, [ch 3 picot in last sc made, 4 sc in same sp] twice, 2 sc in ch-6 sp, ch 3 picot in last sc made, 4 sc in same sp, rep from * across, ending with sc in next sc. Fasten off. Weave in ends.

4. EDGING BULLION SHELLS

SKILL LEVEL

INTERMEDIATE

FINISHED MEASUREMENTS
Each rep = 1 inch wide x ¾ inch tall

MATERIALS
- Size 10 crochet cotton:
   White amount needed varies by
   length of edging
- Size 7/1.65mm steel crochet hook

Note: Edging has multiple of 8 + 1. Sample: 8 x 10 = 80 + 1 = 81 + 1 for turning ch = 82 total.

Use appropriate inline hook for the bullion sts.

Row 1: Ch 82, sc in 2nd ch from hook, sc in each ch across, turn.

Row 2: Ch 1, sc in first sc, sk next 3 sc, ([8-wrap bullion st] 3 times) in next sc, ch-3 picot in top of last bullion st made, (8-wrap bullion st in same sc as previous bullion st) 3 times, sk next 3 sc, *sc in next sc, sk next 3 sc, ([8-wrap bullion st] 3 times) in next sc, ch-3 picot in top of last bullion st made, (8-wrap bullion st in same sc as previous bullion st) 3 times, sk next 3 sc, rep from * across, ending with sc in last sc. Fasten off. Weave in ends.

5. WHEEL EDGING

SKILL LEVEL

INTERMEDIATE

FINISHED MEASUREMENTS
Each rep = 1¾ inches wide x 1⅛ inches tall

MATERIALS
- Size 10 crochet cotton:
   White amount needed varies by
   length of edging
- Size 7/1.65mm steel crochet hook

Note: Edging has multiple of 17 + 1. Sample: 17 x 5 = 85 + 1 = 86 + 2 for turning ch = 88 total.

Row 1: Ch 88, dc in 4th ch from hook, dc in each ch across, turn.

Row 2: Ch 1, sc in first dc, sc in each of next 11 dc, ch 5, turn, sk next 3 dc, sc in next sc, sl st in next sc, ch 1, turn, 7 sc in ch-5 sp, sc in each of next 3 dc, ch 2, turn, sk next 3 sc on base, dc in next sc, [ch 2, dc in next sc] 5 times, ch 2, sk next 2 sc on base, sc in next sc, sl st in next sc, ch 1, turn, [2 sc in next ch-2 sp, ch 3 picot in last sc made, sc in same sp] 7 times, *sc in each of next 14 dc, ch 5, turn, sk next 3 sc, sc in next sc, sl st in next sc, ch 1, turn, 7 sc in ch-5 sp, sc in each of next 3 sc, ch 2, turn, sk next 3 sc on base, dc in next sc, [ch 2, dc in next sc] 5 times, ch 2, sk next 2 sc on base, sc in next sc, sl st in next sc, ch 1, turn, [2 sc in next ch-2 sp, ch 3 picot in last sc made, sc in same sp] 7 times, rep from * across, ending with sc in each of next 3 dc. Fasten off. Weave in ends.

6. INSERTION

SKILL LEVEL

INTERMEDIATE

FINISHED MEASUREMENTS
Each rep = ½ inch wide x 1 inch tall

MATERIALS
- Size 10 crochet cotton:
  White amount needed varies by
  length of edging
- Size 7/1.65mm steel crochet hook

CENTER
Row 1: Ch 7, dc in 7th ch from hook, turn.

Row 2: Ch 1, 3 sc in ch-7 sp, ch 3 picot in last sc made, 3 sc in same sp, turn.

Row 3: Ch 5, sk next 5 sc, dc in next sc, turn.

Row 4: Ch 1, 3 sc in ch-5 sp, ch 3 picot in last sc made, 3 sc in same sp, turn.

Rep rows 3 and 4 until 1 rep from desired length.

Rep row 3.

Row 5: Ch 1, 6 sc in ch-5 sp.

EDGING SIDE A
Row 1: Ch 4, working across side edge of Center, dc in ch sp of previous row, *ch 2, dc in next ch sp, ch 2, dc in same sp, rep from * across long edge of Center, turn.

Row 2: Ch 1, work 2 sc in each ch-2 sp across row 1 of Edging. Fasten off. Weave in ends.

EDGING SIDE B
Row 1 (RS): Join thread over post of dc on row 1 of Center, ch 4, dc over same post, *ch 2, dc over post of next dc, ch 2, dc over same post, rep from * across long edge of Center, turn.

Row 2: Rep row 2 of Edging Side A.

7. EDGING RINGS WITH PICOTS SINGLE JOIN

SKILL LEVEL

INTERMEDIATE

FINISHED MEASUREMENTS
Each rep = 1 inch wide x 1 inch tall

MATERIALS
- Size 10 crochet cotton:
  White amount needed varies by
  length of edging
- Size 7/1.65mm steel crochet hook
- Size G/6/4mm crochet hook for pc

RING 1
Rnd 1: Using nonworking end of size G hook, make 12-wrap pc ring, 16 sc in ring, sl st in first sc in ring; or ch 5, sl st to form ring, ch 1, 16 sc in ring, join in first sc.

Rnd 2: Ch 1, sc in same sc, ch 5, [sc in each of next 2 sc, ch 5] 7 times, ending with sc in next sc, join in first sc. Fasten off. Weave in ends.

RING 2
Rnd 1: Rep rnd 1 of Ring 1.

Rnd 2: Ch 1, sc in same sc, ch 5, [sc in each of next 2 sc, ch 5] 6 times, sc in each of next 2 sc, ch 2, sc in any ch-5 sp on previous ring, ch 2, sc in next sc, join in first sc. Fasten off. Weave in ends.

RING 3
Rnd 1: Rep rnd 1 of Ring 1.

Rnd 2: Ch 1, sc in same sc, ch 5, [sc in each of next 2 sc, ch 5] 6 times, sc in each of next 2 sc, ch 2, sk next 3 ch-5 sps from joining, sc in next ch-5 sp on previous ring, ch 2, sc in next sc, join in first sc. Fasten off. Weave in ends.

Rep Ring 3 until desired length of Edging.

8. EDGING RINGS WITH PICOTS DOUBLE JOIN

SKILL LEVEL

INTERMEDIATE

FINISHED MEASUREMENTS
Each rep = 1⅛ inches wide x 1 inch tall

MATERIALS
- Size 10 crochet cotton:
  White amount needed varies by length of edging
- Size 7/1.65mm steel crochet hook
- Size G/6/4mm crochet hook for pc

RING 1
Rnd 1: Using nonworking end of size G hook, make 12-wrap pc ring, 16 sc in ring, sl st in first sc in ring; or ch 5, sl st to form ring, ch 1, 16 sc in ring, join in first sc.

Rnd 2: Ch 1, sc in same sc, ch 5, [sc in each of next 2 sc, ch 5] 7 times, ending with sc in next sc, join in first sc. Fasten off. Weave in ends.

RING 2
Rnd 1: Rep rnd 1 of Ring 1.

Rnd 2: Ch 1, sc in same sc, ch 5, [sc in each of next 2 sc, ch 5] 5 times, sc in each of next 2 sc, ch 2, sc in any ch-5 sp on previous ring, ch 2, sc in each of next 2 sc, ch 2, sc in next ch-5 sp on previous ring, ch 2, sc in next sc, join in first sc. Fasten off. Weave in ends.

RING 3
Rnd 1: Rep rnd 1 of Ring 1.

Rnd 2: Ch 1, sc in same sc, ch 5, [sc in each of next 2 sc, ch 5] 5 times, sc in each of next 2 sc, ch 2, sk next 2 ch-5 sps from joining, sc in next ch-5 sp on previous ring, ch 2, sc in each of next 2 sc, ch 2, sc in next ch-5 sp on previous ring, ch 2, sc in next sc, join in first sc. Fasten off. Weave in ends.

Rep Ring 3 until desired length of Edging.

9. RINGS WITH PICOTS DOUBLE JOIN & TOP EDGING

SKILL LEVEL

INTERMEDIATE

FINISHED MEASUREMENTS
Each rep = 1⅛ inches x wide 1½ inches tall

MATERIALS
- Size 10 crochet cotton:
  White amount needed varies by length of edging
- Size 7/1.65mm steel crochet hook

Work Edging Rings With Picots Double Join pattern until desired length of edging.

Row 1: Join thread in the 3rd ch-5 lp from the first joining of the first and 2nd ring that will have you working toward the first joining, ch 6 *(counts as first tr, ch 3)*, sc in next ch-5 lp, ch 3, sc in next ch-5 lp, ch 3, tr over next joining, *ch 3, sc in next ch-5 lp, ch 3, sc in next ch 5 lp, ch 3, tr over next joining, rep from * across, ending with ch 3, sc in next ch-5 lp, ch 3, sc in next ch-5 lp, ch 3, tr in next ch-5 lp, turn.

Row 2: Ch 1, sc in first tr, *[3 sc in next ch-3 sp, sc in next sc] twice, 3 sc in next ch-3 sp, sc in next tr, rep from * across, turn.

Row 3: Ch 3 (*counts as first dc, ch 1*), sk next sc, dc in next sc, [ch 1, sk next sc, dc in next sc] across, turn.

Row 4: Ch 1, sc in same dc, [sc in next ch-1 sp, sc in next dc] across. Fasten off. Weave in ends.

10. RINGS WITH PICOTS DOUBLE JOIN INSERTION

SKILL LEVEL
INTERMEDIATE

FINISHED MEASUREMENTS
Each rep = 1⅛ inches wide x 2 inches tall

MATERIALS
- Size 10 crochet cotton: White amount needed varies by length of edging
- Size 7/1.65mm steel crochet hook

Work Edging Rings With Picots Double Join pattern until desired length of edging.

Row 1: Attach white thread in the 3rd ch-5 sp from first joining of the first and 2nd ring that will have you working toward the first joining, ch 6 (*counts as first tr, ch 3*), sc in next ch-5 lp, ch 3, sc in next ch-5 lp, ch 3, tr over next joining, *ch 3, sc in next ch-5 lp, ch 3, sc in next ch-5 lp, ch 3, tr over next joining, rep from * across,

ending with ch 3, sc in next ch-5 lp, ch 3, sc in next ch-5 lp, ch 3, tr in next ch-5 lp, turn.

Row 2: Ch 1, sc in first tr, *[3 sc in next ch-3 sp, sc in next sc] twice, 3 sc in next ch-3 sp, sc in next tr, rep from * across, turn.

Row 3: Ch 3 (*counts as first dc, ch 1*), sk next sc, dc in next sc, [ch 1, sk next sc, dc in next sc] across, turn.

Row 4: Ch 1, sc in same dc, [sc in next ch-1 sp, sc in next dc] across. Fasten off. Weave in ends.

2ND SIDE OF INSERTION
Working on opposite edge, rep rows 1–4.

11. 8-PETAL ROSE EDGING

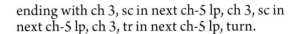

SKILL LEVEL
INTERMEDIATE

FINISHED MEASUREMENTS
Each rep = 2¾ inches wide x 3⅜ inches tall

MATERIALS
- Size 10 crochet cotton: White amount needed varies by length of edging
- Size 7/1.65mm steel crochet hook

MOTIF 1
Ch 5, join to form ring.

Rnd 1: Ch 1, 16 sc in ring, join in first sc.

Rnd 2: Ch 1, sc in same sc, ch 3, sk next sc, [sc in next sc, ch 3, sk next sc] around, join in first sc.

Rnd 3: Ch 1, sc in same sc, (hdc, 3 dc, hdc) in next ch-3 sp *sc in next sc, (hdc, 3 dc, hdc) in next ch-3 sp, rep from * around, join in first sc.

Rnd 4: Ch 1, sc in same sc, [ch 6, sl st in 4th ch from hook for picot] twice, ch 3, *sc in next sc, [ch 6, sl st in 4th ch from hook for picot] twice, ch 3, rep from * around, join in first sc.

Rnd 5: Sl st up to and in ch-3 sp between 2 picots, ch 7 (*counts as first dc, ch 5*), dc in same sp, ch 5, *(dc, ch 5, dc) in next ch-3 sp between 2 picots, ch 5, rep from * around, ending with join in 2nd ch of beg ch-7. Fasten off. Weave in ends. (*16 ch-5 sps*)

MOTIF 2
Rnds 1–4: Rep rnds 1–4 of Motif 1.

Rnd 5: Sl st up to and in ch-3 sp between 2 picots, ch 7, dc in same sp, ch 5, [(dc, ch 5, dc) in next ch-3 sp between the 2 picots, ch 5] 5 times, dc in next ch-3 sp between 2 picots, ch 2, sc in any ch-5 sp on previous motif that is between 2 picots above a petal, ch 2, dc in same sp on working motif, ch 5, dc in next ch-3 sp between 2 picots, ch 2, sk next ch-5 sp on previous motif, sc in next ch-5 sp, ch 2, dc in same sp on working motif, ch 5, join in 2nd ch of beg ch-7. Fasten off. Weave in ends.

MOTIF 3
Rnds 1–4: Rep rnds 1–4 of Motif 1.

Rnd 5: Sl st up to and in ch-3 sp between 2 picots, ch 7, dc in same sp, ch 5, [(dc, ch 5, dc) in next ch-3 sp between 2 picots, ch 5] 5 times, dc in next ch-3 sp between 2 picots, ch 2, sk next 5 ch-5 sps from joining on previous motif, sc in next ch-5 sp on previous motif that is between 2 picots above petal, ch 2, dc in same sp on working motif, ch 5, dc in next ch-3 sp between 2 picots, ch 2, sk next ch-5 sp on previous motif, sc in next ch-5 sp, ch 2, dc in same sp on working motif, ch 5, join in 2nd ch of beg ch-7. Fasten off. Weave in ends.

Rep Motif 3 until desired length of edging.

TOP EDGE
Row 1: With WS facing, join in the 6th ch-5 sp before first motif joining, ch 5, dtr in next ch-5 sp, ch 5, (dc, ch 4, dc) in next ch-5 sp, ch 4, sk next ch-5 sp, (dc, ch 4, dc) in next ch-5 sp, *ch 5, holding the last lp of each st on the hook [dtr in next ch-5 sp] twice, yo, draw through all lps on hook (*dtr joining made*), ch 5, (dc, ch 4, dc) in next ch-5 sp, ch 4, sk next ch-5 sp, (dc, ch 4, dc) in next ch-5 sp, rep from * across, ending with ch 5, holding last lp of each st on hook, dtr in next ch-5 sp, trtr in 3rd ch of next ch-5 sp, yo, draw through all lps on hook, turn.

Row 2: Ch 1, sc in first st, 5 sc in next ch-5 sp, [sc in next dc, 5 sc in next ch-4 sp] 3 times, sc in next dc, *5 sc in next ch-5 sp, sc between the dtr of joining, 5 sc in next ch-5 sp, [sc in next dc, 5 sc in next ch-4 sp] 3 times, sc in next dc, rep from * across, ending with 5 sc in next ch-5 sp, sc in next dtr, turn.

Row 3: Ch 4, sk next 2 sc, dc in next sc, [ch 2, sk next 2 sc, dc in next sc] across, turn.

Row 4: Ch 1, sc in dc, [2 sc in next ch-2 sp, dc in next dc] across. Fasten off. Weave in ends.

LOWER EDGE
Working down side of the edging, 2 sc over post of dc, sc in end of row 2 of Top Edge, 5 sc over post of trtr, 3 sc in next ch-2 sp, 5 sc in next ch-5 sp, 4 sc in next ch-5 sp, hdc in same sp, 4 dc in next ch-5 sp, ch 3 picot in last dc made, 3 dc in same sp, hdc in next ch-5 sp, 2 sc in same sp, ch 3 picot in last sc made, sc in same sp, hdc in same sp, 4 dc in next ch-5 sp, triple picot in last dc made, 3 dc in same sp, hdc in next ch-5 sp, 2 sc in same sp, ch 3 picot in last sc made, sc in same sp, hdc in same sp, 4 dc in next ch-5 sp, ch 3 picot in last dc made, 3 dc in same sp, *hdc in next ch 2 sp, sc in same sp, sc in next ch-2 sp, hdc in same sp, 4 dc in next ch-5 sp, ch 3 picot in last dc made, 3 dc in same sp, hdc in next ch-5 sp, 2 sc in same sp, ch 3 picot in last sc made, sc in same sp, hdc in same sp, 4 dc in next ch-5 sp, triple picot in last dc made, 3 dc in same sp, hdc in next ch-5 sp, 2 sc in same sp, ch 3 picot in last sc made, sc in same sp, hdc in same sp, 4 dc in next ch-5 sp, ch 3 picot in last dc made, 3 dc in same sp, rep from * across, ending with hdc in next ch-5 sp, 4 sc in same sp, 5 sc in next ch-5 sp, 3 sc in next ch-2 sp, 5 sc in next ch-5 sp, sc in end of row 2 of top edging, 2 sc over post of first dc, join in first sc of row 4 of Top Edge. Fasten off. Weave in ends.

12. 8-PETAL ROSE MATCHING INSERTION

SKILL LEVEL

INTERMEDIATE

FINISHED MEASUREMENTS

Each rep = 2¾ inches wide x 3 inches tall

MATERIALS

- Size 10 crochet cotton:
  White amount needed varies by
  length of edging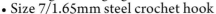
- Size 7/1.65mm steel crochet hook

Rep 8-Petal Rose Edging pattern until desired number of motifs completed.

Rnd 1: With RS facing, join thread in the 7th ch-5 sp before the first Motif joining, ch 1, sc in same sp, ch 5 {sc in next ch-5 sp, ch 5, dtr in next ch-5 sp, ch 5, dc in next ch-5 sp, ch 4, dc in same sp, ch 4, sk next ch-5 sp, dc in next ch-5 sp, ch 4, dc in same sp, *ch 5, dtr joining worked in next 2 ch-5 sps, ch 5, dc in next ch-5 sp, ch 4, dc in same sp, ch 4, sk next ch-5 sp, dc in next ch-5 sp, ch 4, dc in same sp, rep from * across top edge of the insertion, ch 5, dtr in next ch-5 sp, ch 5, sc in next ch-5 sp, ch 5, sc in next ch-5 sp, ch 5} twice, join in first sc. Fasten off. Weave in ends.

Row 1: Now working in rows, with RS facing, join thread in top of first dtr, ch 1, sc in same st, 5 sc in next ch-5 sp, [sc in next dc, 5 sc in next ch-4 sp] 3 times, sc in next dc, *5 sc in next ch-5 sp, sc between the dtr of joining, 5 sc in next ch-5 sp, [sc in next dc, 5 sc in next ch-4 sp] 3 times, sc in next dc, rep from * across, ending with 5 sc in next ch-5 sp, sc in next dtr, turn.

Row 2: Ch 4, sk next 2 sc, dc in next sc, [ch 2, sk next 2 sc, dc in next sc] across to next corner, turn.

Row 3: Ch 1, sc in first st, [2 sc in next ch-2 sp, sc in next dc] across. Fasten off. Weave in ends.

Rep rows 1–3 on opposite side.

13. 6-PETAL ROSE EDGING

SKILL LEVEL

INTERMEDIATE

FINISHED MEASUREMENTS

Each rep = 2 inches wide x 2¼ inches tall

MATERIALS

- Size 10 crochet cotton:
  White amount needed varies by
  length of edging
- Size 7/1.65mm steel crochet hook
- Size G/6/4mm crochet hook for pc

MOTIF 1

Rnd 1: Using nonworking end of a size G hook, with white, make a 12-wrap pc ring, 12 sc in ring, sl st in first sc in ring (traditional); or, ch 5, sl st to form ring (updated), 12 sc in ring, join in first sc.

Rnd 2: Ch 1, sc in same sc, ch 3, sk next sc, [sc in next sc, ch 3, sk next sc] around, join in first sc. (6 ch-3 sps)

Rnd 3: Ch 1, sc in same sc, 5 dc in next ch-3 sp, [sc in next sc, 5 dc in next ch-3 sp] around, join in first sc. (6 petals)

Rnd 4: Ch 4, dc in same sc, ch 7, [(dc, ch 2, dc) in next sc, ch 7] around, join in 2nd ch of beg ch-4. Fasten off. Weave in ends.

MOTIF 2
Rnds 1–3: Rep rnds 1–3 of Motif 1.

Rnd 4: Ch 4, dc in same sc, ch 7, [(dc, ch 2, dc) in next sc, ch 7] 4 times, (dc, ch 2, dc) in next sc, ch 3, sc in any ch-7 sp on previous motif, ch 3, join in 2nd ch of beg ch-4. Fasten off. Weave in ends.

MOTIF 3
Rnds 1–3: Rep rnds 1–3 of Motif 1.

Rnd 4: Ch 4, dc in same sc, ch 7, [(dc, ch 2, dc) in next sc, ch 7] 4 times, (dc, ch 2, dc) in next sc, ch 3, sk next 2 ch-7 sps on previous motif, sc in next ch-7 sp on previous motif, ch 3, join in 2nd ch of beg ch-4. Fasten off. Weave in ends.

Note: *Motif should be directly across from the first motif. All motifs should run in a straight line when attached.*

Rep Motif 3 until desired length.

TOP EDGE
Row 1: With WS facing, join white in the 4th ch of ch-7 sp on end, ch 10, dc in next ch-7 sp, ch 5, dc in next ch-2 sp, *[ch 5, dc in next ch-7 sp] twice, ch 5, dc in next ch-2 sp, rep from * across top edge, ending with ch 5, dc in next ch-7 sp, ch 2, quad tr in the 4th ch of next ch-7 sp, turn.

Row 2: Ch 1, sc in same quad tr, 2 sc in next ch-2 sp, sc in next dc, [5 sc in next ch-5 sp, sc in next dc] across, ending with 2 sc in last ch sp, sc in 8th ch of ch-10 at beg of previous row, turn.

Row 3: Ch 4, sk next 2 sc, dc in next sc, [ch 2, sk next 2 sc, dc in next sc] across, turn.

Row 4: Ch 1, sc in first dc as beg ch-1, [2 sc in next ch-2 sp, sc in next dc] across.

LOWER EDGING
Working down side on end of the edging, 2 sc over dc post, sc in end of row 2, 7 sc over post of quad tr, 3 sc in next ch-3 sp, 2 sc in next ch-2 sp, ch 3 picot in last sc made, sc in same sp, 4 sc in next ch-7 sp, ch 3 picot in last sc made, 3 sc in same sp, *2 sc in next ch-2 sp, ch 3 picot in last sc made, sc in same sp, 4 sc in next ch-7 sp, ch 3 picot in last sc made, 3 sc in same sp, 2 sc in next ch-2 sp, ch 3 picot in last sc made, sc in same sp, [2 sc in next ch-3 sp] twice, 2 sc in next ch-2 sp, ch 3 picot in last sc made, sc in same sp, 4 sc in next ch-7 sp, ch 3 picot in last sc made, 3 sc in same sp, rep from * across, ending with 2 sc in next ch-2 sp, ch 3 picot in last sc made, sc in same sp, 4 sc in next ch-7 sp, ch 3 picot in last sc made, 3 sc in same sp, 2 sc in next ch-2 sp, ch 3 picot in last sc made, sc in same sp, 3 sc in next ch-3 sp, 7 sc in next ch-7 sp. Fasten off. Weave in ends.

14. 6-PETAL ROSE MATCHING INSERTION

SKILL LEVEL

INTERMEDIATE

FINISHED MEASUREMENTS
Each rep = 2 inches wide x 2½ inches tall

MATERIALS

- Size 10 crochet cotton:
  White amount needed varies by length of edging
- Size 7/1.65mm steel crochet hook

Rep Motifs 1–3 of 6-Petal Rose Edging, then rep Motif 3 until desired number of motifs completed.

BORDER
Rnd 1: With RS facing, join white in the end ch-7 sp, ch 1, sc in same sp, ch 10, dc in next ch-7 sp, ch 5, dc in next ch-2 sp, *[ch 5, dc in next ch-7

sp] twice, ch 5, dc in next ch-2 sp, rep from *
across top edge, ending with ch 5, dc in next
ch-7 sp, ch 10, sc in next ch-7 sp, ch 10, dc in
next ch-7 sp, ch 5, dc in next ch-2 sp, **[ch 5, dc
in next ch-7 sp] twice, ch 5, dc in next ch-2 sp,
rep from ** across, ending with ch 5, dc in next
ch-7 sp, ch 10, join in first sc.

Rnd 2: Ch 1, sc in same sc, 11 sc in next ch-10
sp, [sc in next dc, 5 sc in next ch-5 sp] across, sc
in next dc, ending with 11 sc in next ch-10 sp,
sc in next sc, 11 sc in next ch-10 sp, [sc in next
dc, 5 sc in next ch-5 sp] across, sc in next dc,
ending with 11 sc in next ch-10 sp, join in first
sc. Fasten off. Weave in end.

SIDE A

Row 1: With WS facing, join white in the 9th
sc in ch-10 sp, ch 4, sk next 2 sc, dc in next sc,
[ch 2, sk next 2 sc, dc in next sc] across, ending
with last dc worked in 3rd sc in ch-10 sp, turn.

Row 2: Ch 1, sc in same dc, [2 sc in next ch-2 sp,
sc in next dc] across. Fasten off. Weave in end.

SIDE B

Rep rows 1 and 2 on other side of insertion. ∎

Chapter 6 DANGLES

Dangles or embellishments can be used to finish off a piece, add more 3-D interest to a design, or as accents on the edge of a piece. Use them at the end of ties to create a special look. Hang the crocheted Fuchsia shrub from your Christmas tree to make a truly unique ornament.

1. CLOVER DANGLE

SKILL LEVEL

EASY

FINISHED MEASUREMENTS

¾ inch wide x 1 inch long

MATERIALS

- Size 10 crochet cotton:
  5 yds white
- Size 7/1.65mm steel crochet hook

Ch 8, join in 4th ch from hook to form ring, ch 1, sc in ring, (hdc, dc, tr, dc, hdc, sc) 3 times in ring, sl st in each of rem 4 chs of beg ch-8. Fasten off. Weave in ends.

2. SINGLE CROCHET SPIRAL

SKILL LEVEL

EASY

FINISHED MEASUREMENTS

¼ inch wide x 1¾ inches long

MATERIALS

- Size 10 crochet cotton:
  10 yds white
- Size 7/1.65mm steel crochet hook
- Stitch marker

Ch 25, place marker in 10th ch, 3 sc in top lp of 2nd ch from hook, working in top lp of ch, 3 sc in each of next 13 chs, 2 sc in next ch, sl st in same ch, remove marker, sl st in both lps of each rem ch. Fasten off. Weave in ends.

3. DOUBLE CROCHET SPIRAL

SKILL LEVEL

EASY

FINISHED MEASUREMENTS

⅜ inch wide x 2 inches long

MATERIALS

- Size 10 crochet cotton:
  10 yds white
- Size 7/1.65mm steel crochet hook
- Stitch marker

Ch 25, place marker in 10th ch, 3 dc in top lp of 2nd ch from hook, working in top lp of ch, 3 dc in each of next 13 chs, 2 sc in next ch, sl st in same ch, remove marker, sl st in both lps of each rem ch. Fasten off. Weave in ends.

4. BALL DANGLE A

SKILL LEVEL

EASY

FINISHED MEASUREMENTS
1 inch wide x 2 inches long

MATERIALS
- Size 10 crochet cotton:
  15 yds white
- Size 7/1.65mm steel crochet hook
- Scrap of fiberfill

Rnd 1: Ch 4, sl st to form ring, ch 1, 8 sc in ring, join in back lp of first sc.

Rnd 2: Working in back lp unless otherwise stated, ch 1, 2 sc in same sc as beg ch-1, 2 sc in each st around, join in back lp of first sc. *(16 sc)*

Rnd 3: Ch 1, 2 sc in same sc as beg ch-1, sc in next sc, [2 sc in next sc, sc in next sc] around, join in back lp of first sc. *(24 sc)*

Rnds 4–9: Ch 1, sc in same sc, sc in each sc around, join in back lp of first sc.

Rnd 10: [Sc dec over next 2 sc, sc in next sc] around, join in first sc. Stuff Ball with fiberfill. *(16 sc)*

Rnds 11 & 12: [Sc dec over next 2 sc] around, join in first sc. *(4 sc)*

Ch 11, sl st in 2nd ch from hook, sl st in each of next 9 ch sts, sl st in top of Ball. Fasten off. Weave in ends.

5. BALL DANGLE B

SKILL LEVEL

EASY

FINISHED MEASUREMENTS
⅞ inch wide x 1¾ inches long

MATERIALS
- Size 10 crochet cotton:
  15 yds white
- Size 7/1.65mm steel crochet hook
- Scrap of fiberfill

Rnd 1: Ch 4, sl st to form ring, ch 1, 8 sc in ring, join in first sc.

Rnd 2: Ch 1, 2 sc in same sc as beg ch-1, 2 sc in each st around, join first sc. *(16 sc)*

Rnd 3: Ch 1, 2 sc in same sc as beg ch-1, sc in next sc, [2 sc in next sc, sc in next sc] around, join in first sc. *(24 sc)*

Rnds 4–9: Ch 1, sc in same sc, sc in each sc around, join in first sc.

Rnd 10: [Sc dec over next 2 sc, sc in next sc] around, join in first sc. Stuff Ball with fiberfill. *(16 sc)*

Rnds 11 & 12: [Sc dec over next 2 sc] around, join in first sc. *(4 sc)*

Ch 11, sl st in 2nd ch from hook, sl st in each of next 9 ch sts, sl st in top of Ball. Fasten off. Weave in ends.

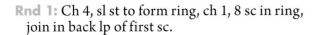
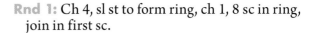

6. BULLION STITCH BEAD

SKILL LEVEL

INTERMEDIATE

FINISHED MEASUREMENTS
⅞ inch wide x 1½ inches long

MATERIALS
- Size 10 crochet cotton:
  15 yds white
- Size 7/1.65mm steel crochet hook
- Scrap of fiberfill

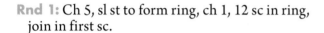

Rnd 1: Ch 5, sl st to form ring, ch 1, 12 sc in ring, join in first sc.

Rnd 2: Ch 1, sc in same st, 2 sc in next sc, [sc in next sc, 2 sc in next sc] around, join in first sc. *(18 sc)*

Rnd 3: Ch 1, sc in same st, sc in each sc around, join in first sc.

Rnd 4: Ch 3, 9-wrap bullion st in same st as beg ch-3, 9-wrap bullion st in each sc around, join in top of first bullion st.

Rnd 5: Ch 1, sc in same bullion st, sc in top of each bullion st around, join in first sc.

Rnd 6: Ch 1, sc in same sc as beg ch-1, sc dec over next 2 sc, [sc in next sc, sc dec over next 2 sc] around, join in first sc. Stuff Bead with fiberfill. *(12 sc)*

Rnd 7: Ch 1, [sc dec over next 2 sc] around, sl st in first sc. Leaving 20-inch length, fasten off, weave tail between each st of rnd 7, gently draw up until top is completely closed, pull thread up through center of closure, ch 10, sl st in each ch st back down to bead, sl st in bead. Fasten off. Weave in end.

7. ACORN

SKILL LEVEL

INTERMEDIATE

FINISHED MEASUREMENTS
¾ inch wide x 1⅝ inches long

MATERIALS
- Size 10 crochet cotton:
  20 yds white
- Size 7/1.65mm steel crochet hook
- White seed bead
- Scrap of fiberfill

ACORN

Rnd 1: Ch 4, join to form ring, ch 1, 8 sc in ring, join in first sc.

Rnd 2: Ch 1, 2 sc in first sc, sc in next sc, [2 sc in next sc, sc in next sc] around, join in first sc. *(12 sc)*

Rnd 3: Ch 1, sc in each sc around, join in first sc.

Rnd 4: Rep rnd 2. *(18 sc)*

Rnds 5–9: Rep rnd 3.

Rnd 10: Ch 1, sc dec over next 2 sc, sc in next sc, [sc dec over next 2 sc, sc in next sc] around, join in first sc. Stuff Acorn firmly with fiberfill. *(12 sc)*

Rnd 11: Ch 1, [sc dec over next 2 sc] around, join in first sc. *(6 sc)*

Rnd 12: Now working on stem, ch 1, [sc in each of next 6 sc, do not join] rep around until Stem is ¾ inch long or desired length, join in next st. Fasten off. Weave in ends.

ACORN CAP

Rnd 1: Ch 8, join to form a ring, ch 1, 16 sc in ring, join in first sc.

Rnd 2: Ch 3, dc in same sc (beg V-st), sk next sc, [(dc, ch 1, dc) in next sc, sk next sc] around, join in 2nd ch of beg ch-3. *(8 V-sts)*

Rnd 3: Sl st in ch-1 sp, ch 1, sc in same ch-1 sp, ch 2, [sc in next ch-1 sp, ch 2] around, join in first sc.

Rnd 4: Sl st in first ch-2 sp, ch 1, (2 sc, ch-3 picot, sc) in same ch-2 sp, [(2 sc, ch-3 picot, sc) in next ch-2 sp] around, join in first sc. Leaving 7-inch length, fasten off.

ASSEMBLY

Insert Stem through starting ring of the Acorn Cap, pull down snug over Acorn base, sew cap on at sc between the picots. When this is complete, pass the needle and thread down through body of the Acorn to the very bottom of the acorn. String bead on thread, work several small sts to secure bead, pass needle back through the Acorn body once to secure and cut thread close to the Acorn.

8. FUCHSIA

SKILL LEVEL

INTERMEDIATE

FINISHED MEASUREMENTS

1¾ inches wide x 4 inches long

MATERIALS

• Size 10 crochet cotton: 50 yds white
• Size 7/1.65mm steel crochet hook
• Scrap of fiberfill

PISTILS

Rnd 1: Ch 4, join to form ring, ch 1, 6 sc in ring, join in first sc.

Rnd 2: Ch 15, dc in 3rd ch from hook, ch 2, sl st in same ch, sl st in each of next 12 chs, sl st in next sc, ch 17, dc in 3rd ch from hook, ch 2, sl st in same ch, sl st in each of next 14 chs, [sl st in next sc, ch 15, dc in 3rd ch from hook, ch 2, sl st in same ch, sl st in each of next 12 chs, sl st in next sc, ch 17, dc in 3rd ch from hook, ch 2, sl st in same ch, sl st in each of next 14 chs] twice, ending with sl st in base of first pistil. Leaving 6-inch length, fasten off. Set aside until just before 11th row of 4th Inner Petal.

Sew facing downward in center of inside of Fuchsia.

STEM

Rnd 1: Ch 2, 5 sc in 2nd ch from hook, join in back lp of first sc.

Note: *Work in back lp of each sc of Stem. Join with sl st in back lp of each sc rnd of Stem.*

Rnds 2–8: Ch 1, sc in same sc, sc in each of next 4 sc, join in first sc.

Rnd 9: Ch 1, 2 sc in same sc, [2 sc in next sc] 4 times, join first sc. *(10 sc)*

Rnd 10: Ch 1, sc in same sc, sc in each of next 9 sc, join in first sc. Stuff Stem with fiberfill.

Rnd 11: Sc dec over first 2 sc, [sc dec over next 2 sc] 4 times, join in first sc. *(5 sc)*

Rnds 12 & 13: Ch 1, sc in each of next 5 sc, join in first sc.

Rnd 14: Rep rnd 9. *(10 sc)*

Rnd 15: Ch 1, 2 sc in same sc, sc in next sc, [2 sc in next sc, sc in next sc] 3 times, 2 sc in each of next 2 sc, join in first sc. *(16 sc)*

Rnds 16 & 17: Ch 1, sc in each of next 16 sc, join in first sc.

Rnd 18: Sc dec over first 2 sc, [sc dec over next 2 sc] 7 times, join in first sc. *(8 sc)*

Rnd 19: Sc dec over first 2 sc, [sc dec over next 2 sc] 3 times, join in first sc. *(4 sc)*

Rnd 20: Ch 1, sc in same sc, [ch 3, sc in next sc] 3 times, ch 3, join in first sc.

TOP PETAL 1

Row 1: Sl st in first ch-3 sp, ch 1, 4 sc in same sp, turn.

Row 2: Ch 1, 2 sc in first sc, sc in each of next 2 sc, 2 sc in next sc, turn. *(6 sc)*

Row 3: Ch 1, 2 sc in first sc, sc in each of next 4 sc, 2 sc in next sc, turn. *(8 sc)*

Row 4: Ch 1, sc in each sc across, turn.

Row 5: Sc dec over first 2 sc, sc in each of next 4 sc, sc dec over next 2 sc, turn. *(6 sc)*

Row 6: Sc dec over first 2 sc, sc in each of next 2 sc, sc dec over next 2 sc, turn. *(4 sc)*

Row 7: [Sc dec over next 2 sc] twice, turn. *(2 sc)*

Row 8: Sc dec over next 2 sc, turn.

Row 9: Sl st down side of Petal, sl st in same ch-3 sp.

PETALS 2–4

Row 1: Sl st in next ch-3 sp, ch 1, 4 sc in same sp, turn.

Rows 2–9: Rep rows 2–9 of Top Petal 1.

INNER PETALS

Foundation rnd: On inside of Petals, sl st from ch-3 sp of rnd 20 up to and between 2nd and 3rd sc of Top Petal 1, ch 1, sc in same sp, ch 4, [sc between 2nd and 3rd sc on next petal, ch 4] 3 times, join in first sc.

INNER PETAL 1

Row 1: Sl st in first ch-4 sp, ch 1, 8 sc in same sp, turn. *(8 sc)*

Row 2: Ch 1, 2 sc in first sc, sc in each of next 6 sc, 2 sc in next sc, turn. *(10 sc)*

Row 3: Ch 1, 2 sc in first sc, sc in each of next 8 sc, 2 sc in next sc, turn. *(12 sc)*

Rows 4–10: Ch 1, sc in each sc across, turn.

Row 11: Sc dec over first 2 sc, sc in next sc, sc dec over next 2 sc, sc in each of next 2 sc, sc dec over next 2 sc, sc in next sc, sc dec over next 2 sc. *(8 sc)*

Row 12: Sl st down side of Petal, sl st in same ch-4 sp.

INNER PETALS 2 & 3

Row 1: Sl st in next ch-4 sp, ch 1, 8 sc in same sp, turn. *(8 sc)*

Rows 2–10: Rep Rows 2–10 of Inner Petal 1. At the end of row 10, do not turn.

Row 11: Sl st between the 2 sc in middle of row 11 on the previous Petal, turn, sc dec over first 2 sc on working petal, sc in next sc, sc dec over next 2 sc, sc in each of next 2 sc, sc dec over next 2 sc, sc in next sc, sc dec over next 2 sc.

Row 12: Sl st down side of petal, sl st in same ch-4 sp.

INNER PETAL 4

Rows 1–10: Sl st in next ch-4 sp, rep rows 1–10 of Inner Petal 1. Sew Pistils in place at this time, facing downward in center of inside of Fuchsia.

Row 11: Sl st between 2 sc in middle of row 11 on previous petal, turn, sc dec over first 2 sc on working petal, sc in next sc, sc dec over next 2 sc, sc in next sc, sl st in first dec st of row 11 on first petal, sc in next sc on working petal, sc dec over next 2 sc, sc in next sc, sc dec over next 2 sc.

Row 12: Sl st down side of petal, sl st in same ch-4 sp. Fasten off. Weave in ends. ∎

Chapter 7 OVERLAYS

Overlay designs involve layering different components to make one motif. Each element is worked separately and then sewn together. This allows a greater creative license in the motifs. It is fun to take different motifs and put them together to make a whole new design. Try experimenting with the motifs in this book or use the ones I have provided as a jumping-off point.

1. 6-POINT FLOWER: TRADITIONAL PC & PR

SKILL LEVEL

INTERMEDIATE

FINISHED MEASUREMENT
5 inches across

MATERIALS
- Size 10 crochet cotton:
  30 yds white
- Size 7/1.65mm steel crochet hook
- Sewing needle
- Matching sewing thread
- Size G/6/4mm crochet hook for pc

Padding cord lengths: Cut 2 lengths of white each 5 feet long for padding cord, hold tog and fold in half, wrap on padding cord bobbin.

Rnd 1: Using nonworking end of size G hook, with white, make a 12-wrap pc ring, 12 sc in ring, join in first sc.

Rnd 2: Ch 2, dc in same sc, 2 dc in each sc around, join in 2nd ch of beg ch-2. *(24 dc)*

Rnd 3: Ch 1, sc in same dc, sc in each of next 2 dc, 2 sc in next dc, [sc in each of next 3 dc, 2 sc in next dc] around, join in first sc. *(30 sc)*

PETALS
PETAL 1
Row 1 (RS): Ch 4, sk next sc, 3 dc in next sc, ch 2, sk next sc, dc in next sc, turn.

Row 2: Ch 4, 2 dc in next dc, bpdc in next dc, 2 dc in next dc, ch 2, dc in 2nd ch of beg ch-4, turn.

Row 3: Ch 4, 2 dc in next dc, dc in next dc, fpdc in next bpdc, dc in next dc, 2 dc in next dc, ch 2, dc in 2nd ch of beg ch-4, turn.

Row 4: Ch 4, dc dec over next 2 dc, dc in next dc, bpdc in next fpdc, dc in next dc, dec dc over next 2 dc, ch 2, dc in 2nd ch of beg ch-4, turn.

Row 5: Ch 4, dc dec over next 2 dc, fpdc in next bpdc, dc dec over next 2 dc, ch 2, dc in 2nd ch of beg ch-4, turn.

Row 6: Ch 4, holding last lp of each st on the hook, dc in next dc, bpdc in next fpdc, dc in next dc, yo, draw through all lps on hook *(cluster made)*, ch 2, dc in 2nd ch of beg ch-4, turn.

Row 7: Ch 5, sl st in 2nd ch of beg ch-4 at beg of previous row. Fasten off. Weave in ends.

PETALS 2-6
Row 1: With RS facing, join thread in next sc on rnd 3, ch 4, sk next sc, 3 dc in next sc, ch 2, sk next sc, dc in next sc, turn.

Rows 2-7: Rep Rows 2-7 of Petal 1.

Rnd 8: Now working in rnds, join thread in first ch-2 sp on side of petal and working toward tip of petal over end sp of each row *(ch-2 sp or* *dc)*, sl st in fold of padding cord, work over all 4 strands of padding cord unless otherwise noted, ch 1, 3 sc in same sp, 3 sc in next sp, [(sc, hdc, dc, hdc, sc) in next sp] 4 times, sc in next ch-5 sp, (hdc, dc, hdc, sc) 3 times in same ch-5 sp, (sc, hdc, dc, hdc, sc in next sp) 4 times, [(3 sc in next sp) 4 times, (sc, hdc, dc, sl st in last dc on previous petal, hdc, sc) in next sp, (sc, hdc, dc, hdc, sc in next sp) 3 times, sc in next ch-5 sp, (hdc, dc, hdc, sc) 3 times in same ch-5 sp, (sc, hdc, dc, hdc, sc in next sp) 4 times] 4 times, (3 sc in next sp) 4 times, (sc, hdc, dc, sl st in last dc on previous petal, hdc, sc) in same ch sp, (sc, hdc, dc, hdc, sc in next sp) 3 times, sc in next ch-5 sp, (hdc, dc, hdc, sc) 3 times in same ch-5 sp, (sc, hdc, dc, hdc, sc in same sp) 3 times, sc in next sp, hdc, dc, sl st in first dc on first petal, hdc, sc in same sp, (3 sc in next sp) twice, join in first sc. Fasten off. Weave in ends.

TENDRIL
MAKE 3.
Ch 18, 3 sc in top lp of 2nd ch from hook, 3 sc in top lp of each of next 2 ch sts, (sc in top lp of next ch, 3 sc in top lp of each of next 2 chs) 3 times, sl st in each of next 5 ch sts *(stem)*. Fasten off. Weave in ends.

CENTER
Using nonworking end of a size G hook, with white, make 12-wrap pc ring, sc in ring, ch 3, (2 sc in ring, ch 3) 5 times, sc in ring, join in first sc. Fasten off. Weave in end.

SCROLL LOOPS LAYER
Ch 70, sl st in 2nd ch from hook, sl st in each ch across *(this should be more than needed but better too many than not enough)*, do not fasten off at this point.

ASSEMBLY
Arrange tendrils facing outward around center of flower. Using sewing needle and thread, sew stem end of each in place. Arrange Scroll Loops on center of flower, forming lps of cord in an even manner and using care that tendrils are under Scroll Loops. Start sewing in place at the closed end of the cord. If you have too many sts, pull out the ones not needed and pick out the extra ch sts. Weave in cord ends. Sew Center in place over Scroll Loops. Fasten off. Weave in ends.

2A. WILD ROSE: TRADITIONAL PC & PR

SKILL LEVEL
INTERMEDIATE

FINISHED MEASUREMENT
4⅝ inches across

MATERIALS
- Size 20 crochet cotton: 50 yds white
- 12 yds size 10 white crochet cotton (padding cord)
- Size 7/1.65mm steel crochet hook
- Sewing needle
- Matching sewing thread
- Sizes G/6/4mm and H/8/5mm crochet hooks for pc

Padding cord lengths: Cut 2 lengths of white size 10 thread 4 yds long for padding cord, hold tog and fold in half, wrap on padding cord bobbin.

Rnd 1: Using the nonworking end of size H hook, make 12-wrap pc ring, 20 sc in ring, join in front lp of first sc.

Rnd 2: Ch 1, sc in same sc, working in front lp around, ch 5, [sc in next sc, ch 5] around, join in first sc.

Rnd 3: Sl st in back lp of first sc of rnd 1, working in back lp around, ch 5 *(counts as first tr, ch 2)*, [tr in next sc, ch 2] around, join in 3rd ch of beg ch-5. *(20 tr, 20 ch-2 sps)*

Rnd 4: Sl st in next ch-2 sp and in fold of padding cord, work over all 4 strands of padding cord unless otherwise noted, ch 1, 3 sc in same ch-2 sp, [3 sc in next ch-2 sp] around, join in first sc, drop padding cord. *(60 sc)*

PETAL 1
Row 1: Now working in rows, ch 1, sc in same st, [ch 3, sc in next sc] 9 times, turn. *(10 sc)*

Rows 2–7: Ch 4, sc in first ch-3 sp, [ch 3, sc in next ch-3 sp] 8 times, turn. Fasten off.

PETALS 2–5
Row 1: Sk next 2 sc on rnd 4, join white in next sc, ch 1, sc in same sc, [ch 3, sc in next sc] 9 times, turn.

Rows 2–7: Rep rows 2–7 of Petal 1.

EDGING
Working on Petal 1, join white in last sc of rnd 4, ch 1, sc in same sc, pick up padding cord, [(sc, 3 dc, sc) in next ch sp on side of petal] 3 times, [(sc, 3 dc, sc) in next ch-3 sp on top edge of petal] 9 times, [(sc, 3 dc, sc) in next ch sp on side of petal] 3 times.

Working on Petals 2–5, *sc in each of next 2 sc on rnd 4, [(sc, 3 dc, sc) in next ch sp on side of petal] 3 times, [(sc, 3 dc, sc) in next ch-3 sp on top edge of petal] 9 times, [(sc, 3 dc, sc) in next ch sp on side of petal] 3 times, rep from * 3 more times, sc in next sc on rnd 4, join in first sc. Fasten off. Weave in ends.

RINGS
MAKE 10.
Using nonworking end of size G hook, with white, make a 12-wrap pc ring, 16 sc in ring, join in first sc. Fasten off. Weave in ends. With needle and sewing thread, sew rings evenly around top of rnd 4 of Flower.

2B. WILD ROSE: UPDATED

SKILL LEVEL

INTERMEDIATE

FINISHED MEASUREMENT
4⅝ inches across

MATERIALS
- Size 20 crochet cotton:
  50 yds white
- Size 7/1.65mm steel crochet hook
- Sewing needle
- Matching sewing thread
- Size G/6/4mm crochet hook for pc

Rnd 1: Ch 6, join to form ring, ch 1, 20 sc in ring, join in front lp of first sc.

Rnd 2: Ch 1, sc in same sc, working in front lp, ch 5, [sc in next sc, ch 5] around, join in first sc.

Rnd 3: Sl st in back lp of first sc of rnd 1, working in back lp, ch 5 *(counts as first tr, ch 2)*, [tr in next sc, ch 2] around, join in 3rd ch of beg ch-5. *(20 tr, 20 ch-2 sps)*

Rnd 4: Sl st in next ch-2 sp, ch 1, 3 sc in same ch-2 sp, [3 sc in next ch-2 sp] around, join in first sc. *(60 sc)*

Rnd 5: Ch 1, sc in each sc around, join in first sc.

PETAL 1

Row 1: Now working in rows, ch 1, sc in same sc, [ch 3, sc in next sc] 9 times, turn.

Row 2–7: Ch 4, sc in first ch 3 sp, [ch 3, sc in next ch-3 sp] 8 times, turn. Fasten off.

PETALS 2–5

Row 1: Sk next 2 sc on rnd 5 of ring, join white in next sc, ch 1, sc in same sc, [ch 3, sc in next sc] 9 times, turn.

Rows 2–7: Rep rows 2–7 of Petal 1.

EDGING

Working on Petal 1, join white in last sc of rnd 5, ch 1, sc in same sc, [(sc, 3 dc, sc) in next ch sp on side of petal] 3 times, [(sc, 3 dc, sc) in next ch-3 sp on top edge of petal] 9 times, [(sc, 3 dc, sc) in next ch sp on side of petal] 3 times.

Working on Petals 2–5, *sc in each of next 2 sc on rnd 5, [(sc, 3 dc, sc) in next ch sp on side of petal] 3 times, [(sc, 3 dc, sc) in next ch-3 sp on top edge of petal] 9 times, [(sc, 3 dc, sc) in next ch sp on side of petal] 3 times, rep from * 3 more times, sc in next sc on rnd 5, join in first sc. Fasten off. Weave in ends.

RINGS
MAKE 10.

Using nonworking end of size G hook, with white, make a 12-wrap pc ring, 16 sc in ring, join in first sc. Fasten off. Weave in ends. With needle and sewing thread, sew rings evenly around top of rnd 5 of Flower.

3. 4-LAYER FLOWER

SKILL LEVEL

INTERMEDIATE

FINISHED MEASUREMENT
6½ inches across

MATERIALS
- Size 20 crochet cotton: 100 yds white
- Size 10 crochet cotton: 16 yds white
- Size 7/1.65mm steel crochet hook
- Sewing needle

- Matching sewing thread
- Size G/6/4mm crochet hook for pc

Padding cord lengths:

Flower Part B: Cut 2 lengths of white size 10 thread
7 feet long for padding cord, hold tog and fold in half, wrap on padding cord bobbin.

Flower Part C: Cut 2 lengths of white size 10 thread
8 feet long for padding cord, hold tog and fold in half, wrap on padding cord bobbin.

Flower Part D: Cut 2 lengths of white size 10 thread
8 feet long for padding cord, hold tog and fold in half, wrap on padding cord bobbin. Cut 2 lengths of white size 10 thread 4 yds long for padding cord, hold tog and fold in half, wrap on padding cord bobbin.

CENTER FLOWER A

Using the nonworking end of a size G hook, with white size 20 thread, make a 12-wrap pc ring, sc in ring, ch 3, (2 sc in ring, ch 3) 5 times, sc in ring, join in first sc. Fasten off. Weave in end.

Note: *This center can be used on any one of the motifs used on B, C or D motifs to make single-layer flowers. You can also use it on B and C motifs to make a medium-size flower of 3 layers.*

SMALL FLOWER PART B

This flower can be used alone as a Small Flower or used with the Medium Flower to make a medium-size flower or with the Medium and Large Flowers to make a 4-Layer Flower.

PETAL 1

Row 1: Catch up white through the fold of 7-foot padding cord, ch 1, 11 sc worked over all 4 strands of padding cord, adjust tension of cord as needed, work over all 4 strands of padding cord unless otherwise noted throughout, turn.

Row 2: Drop padding cord, sc in each of next 2 sc, dc in each of next 6 sc, sc in each of next 3 sc, turn.

Row 3: Sc in each of next 3 sc, sc in each of next 6 dc, sc in each of next 2 sc.

Row 4: Pick up padding cord, work 3 sc over padding cord only, turn, sc in each of next 11 sc sts on row 3, turn.

PETALS 2–7

Row 1: Sc in each of next 6 sc, 5 sc over padding cord only, turn.

Rows 2–4: Rep rows 2–4 of Petal 1.

CENTER

When 7 petals are complete, sc in padding cord, turn at the base of each petal, working fairly tightly to make a small center. Adjust padding cord to draw up center. Leaving a 7-inch length, fasten off.

Thread rem length on sewing needle and sew the first and last petal tog from center outward up to the 6th sc.

MEDIUM FLOWER PART C

Note: *This flower can be used alone as a medium-size flower if you add a padding cord center to flower or used with the Small Flower and the Center to make a 3-layer flower.*

PETAL 1

Row 1: Catch up white thread through the fold of 8-foot padding cord, ch 1, 20 sc worked over all 4 strands of padding cord, adjust tension of cord as needed, work over all 4 strands of padding cord unless otherwise noted throughout, turn.

Row 2: Drop padding cord, sc in first sc, [ch 3, sk next 2 sc, sc in next sc] 5 times leaving rem 4 sc unworked, turn.

Row 3: Sc in first ch-3 sp, [ch 2, sc in next ch-3 sp] 4 times, ch 2, sc in first sc of row 2, turn.

Row 4: Pick up padding cord, work 3 sc over padding cord only, turn, 3 sc in each of next 5 ch-2 sps, sc in next sc of row 3, sc in each of next 4 rem sc from row 1, turn.

PETALS 2–9

Row 1: Sc in each of next 10 sc, 10 sc over padding cord only, turn.

Rows 2–4: Rep rows 2–4 of Petal 1, when 9 petals are complete, sc in padding cord at the base of each petal, working fairly tightly to make a small center. Adjust padding cord to draw up center. Leaving a 7-inch length, fasten off.

Thread rem length on sewing needle and sew the first and last petal tog from center outward up to the 10th sc.

LARGE FLOWER PART D
PETAL 1

Row 1: Ch 23, sc in 5th ch from hook, [ch 2, sk next ch, sc in next ch] 8 times, turn.

Row 2: Sc in first ch-2 sp, [ch 2, sc in next ch-2 sp] 7 times, ch 2, sc in next ch sp, turn.

Row 3: Ch 3, sc in first ch-2 sp, [ch 2, sc in next ch-2 sp] 7 times, ch 2, sc in next sc, sc in each of next 2 ch sts, **do not fasten off.**

PETALS 2–6

Rows 1–3: Rep rows 1–3 of Petal 1, at the end of the 6th petal, sl st in base of first petal, turn.

Rnd 1: Now working in rnds, ch 1, sc in same sp and in fold of the 10-foot padding cord, work over all 4 strands of padding cord unless otherwise noted, for Petal 1, sk next sc, sc in next sc, sk next sc, [3 sc in next ch-2 sp] 8 times, 3 sc in next ch-3 sp, 5 sc over padding cord only, 3 sc in next ch-3 sp, [3 sc in next ch-2 sp] 7 times, sc in next ch-2 sp, sk next sc, sc in next sc, sk next sc.

For Petals 2–6, sc in sp between petals, sk next sc, sc in next sc, sk next sc, [3 sc in next ch-1 sp] 8 times, 3 sc in next ch-3 sp, 5 sc over padding cord only, 3 sc in next ch-3 sp, [3 sc in next ch-2 sp] 7 times, sc in next ch-2 sp, sk next sc, sc in next sc, sk next sc. At the end of Petal 6, join in first sc. Fasten off. Weave in ends.

Rnd 2: For Petal 1, join thread in the 9th sc on any petal, now working toward tip of the petal, ch 3, sk next sc, dc in next sc, [ch 1, sk next sc, dc in next sc] 10 times, ch 1, dc in same sc, [ch 1, sk next sc, dc in next sc] 11 times.

For Petals 2–6, sk next 15 sc, dc in next sc, [ch 1, sk next sc, dc in next sc] 11 times, ch 1, dc in same sc, [ch 1, sk next sc, dc in next sc] 11 times. At end of Petal 6, join in 2nd ch of ch-3.

Rnd 3: For Petal 1, join in first ch-1 sp and in fold of 4 yds padding cord, work over all 4 strands of padding cord, ch 1, sc in same sp, sc in next ch-1 sp, [sc in next ch-1 sp, ch-3 picot in last sc made, sc in same sp] 9 times, 2 sc in next ch-1 sp, ch-3 picot in last sc made, sc in same sp, [sc in next ch-1 sp, ch-3 picot in last sc made, sc in same sp] 9 times.

For Petals 2–6, sc in each of next 4 ch-1 sps, [sc in next ch-1 sp, ch-3 picot in last sc made, sc in same sp] 9 times, 2 sc in next ch-1 sp, ch-3 picot in last sc made, sc in same sp, [sc in next ch-1 sp, ch-3 picot in last sc made, sc in same sp] 9 times, ending last petal with sc in each of next 2 ch-1 sps, join in first sc. Fasten off. Weave in ends.

FLOWER ASSEMBLY FOR 4-LAYER FLOWER
Make all 4 parts A, B, C and D per instructions.

Sew tog, layering from top to bottom A, B, C and D to create motif shown.

This is a versatile design and the 4 layers can be made and sewn together in different combinations to create more flowers that can be used with the 4-Layer Flower or by themselves.

4. FLOWER 5-LAYER ROSE

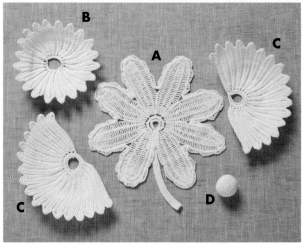

FINISHED MEASUREMENTS
7 inches across x 1⅜ inches tall

MATERIALS
- Size 20 crochet cotton:
  250 yds white
- Size 10 crochet cotton:
  26 yds white
- Size 9/1.25mm steel crochet hook
- Sewing needle

0
LACE

- Matching sewing thread
- Scrap of fiberfill

Padding cord lengths:

Part A: Cut 2 lengths of white size 10 thread 5 yds long for padding cord, hold tog and fold in half, wrap on padding cord bobbin. Cut 3 lengths of white size 10 thread 3 yds long for padding cord, hold tog and fold in half, wrap on padding cord bobbin.

Part B: [Cut 2 lengths of white size 10 thread 17 feet long for padding cord, hold tog and fold in half, wrap on padding cord bobbin] twice.

Part C: Cut 2 lengths of white size 10 thread 6 yds long for padding cord, hold tog and fold in half, wrap on padding cord bobbin.

ROSE BASE PART A
STEM
Row 1: Catch up thread through the fold of 5-yd padding cord, ch 1, 75 sc worked over all 4 strands of padding cord, adjust tension of cord as needed, work over all 4 strands of padding cord unless otherwise noted throughout, turn.

Rows 2 & 3: Ch 1, sc in each sc across, adjust padding cord tension frequently, turn.

Ring: Sl st in center row of Stem on the end, work 25 sc over padding cord, adjust padding cord, sl st in same st on center row of Stem *(ring made)*, turn, working over all 4 strands of padding cord, 15 sc over cord only, sl st in first ring in 9th sc, 15 sc over cord only, sl st in first ring in 18th sc of the first ring, 15 sc over padding cord only. Adjust padding cord, join in the base of first ring, turn.

PETAL 1
Row 1: Work (6 sc, 27 dc, 3 sc) over padding cord only, drop padding cord, turn. *(36 sts)*

Row 2: Ch 1, working over backside of padding cord and through each st, sc in each of next 3 sc, dc in each of next 3 dc, tr in each of next 24 dc, dc in each of next 3 sc, sc in each of next 3 sc, turn.

Row 3: Ch 1, sc in each of next 3 sc, dc in each of next 3 dc, tr in each of next 24 tr, dc in each of next 3 dc, sc in each of next 3 sc, pick up padding cord, work 1 sc over padding cord, turn.

Row 4: Sc in each of next 3 sc, dc in each of next 3 dc, tr in each of next 21 tr, dc in each of next 3 tr, sc in the each of next 3 dc, sc in each of next 3 sc, sk 5 sc on ring, sc in the next sc, turn.

PETAL 2
Row 1: Ch 1, working over padding cord, 1 sc in each of next 6 sc on previous petal, dc in each of next 3 dc, dc in each of next 3 tr, (21 dc, 3 sc) over padding cord only, adjust padding cord, drop padding cord, turn.

Row 2: Ch 1, sc in each of next 3 sc, dc in each of next 3 dc, tr in each of next 24 dc, dc in each of next 3 sc, sc in each of next 3 sc, turn.

Rows 3 & 4: Rep rows 3 and 4 of Petal 1.

PETALS 3–8
Rows 1–4: Rep rows 1–4 of Petal 2. At the end of the 8th Petal, leaving a length to weave in, fasten off padding cord.

EDGING
For Petal 8, ch 1, turn, sc in first sc and through fold of the 3-strand padding cord, working over all 6 strands of padding cord across *(adjust padding cord frequently while working petals)*, dc in each of next 5 sc, dc in each of next 3 dc, [sc in next tr, dc in each of next 8 tr] twice, sc in next tr, dc in each of next 2 tr, dc in each of next 3 dc, dc in each of next 3 sc, sc in sc at tip of petal, working over padding cord and through base of each st on row 1 of petal, 2 dc in next sc, dc in each of next 2 sc, dc in each of next 3 dc, sc in next dc, dc in each of next 7 dc, sc in next dc, dc in each of next 5 dc, sc in next dc, 2 sc over padding cord only.

For Petals 7–2, sk first tr on next petal, [sc in next tr, dc in each of next 7 tr] twice, dc in each of next 3 dc, dc in each of next 3 sc, dc in same dc, sc in sc on tip of petal, working over padding cord and through base of each st on row 1 of petal, 2 dc in next sc, dc in each of next 2 sc, dc in each of next 3 dc, sc in next dc, sc in each of

next 7 dc, sc in next dc, dc in each of next 6 dc, sc in next dc, 2 sc over padding cord only.

For Petal 1, sk first tr on next petal, [sc in next tr, dc in each of next 7 tr] twice, dc in each of next 3 dc, dc in each of next 3 sc, dc in same dc, sc in sc on tip of petal, 2 dc in next sc, dc in each of next 2 dc, dc in each of next 5 dc, sc in next dc, [dc in each of next 8 dc, sc in next dc] twice, dc in each of next 3 dc, dc in each of next 5 sc, sc in next sc, join in first sc of first petal. Fasten off. Weave in ends.

PART B
RING
Work 60 sc over padding cord, join to form ring, adjust padding cord to get the size ring desired.

PETAL 1
Row 1: Working over padding cord alone, work sc and 24 hdc, adjust padding cord tension frequently throughout, turn.

Row 2: Working over padding cord throughout piece, sk hdc, sc in next hdc, hdc in next hdc, dc in each of next 20 hdc, hdc in next hdc, sc in next sc, sc over padding cord only, sk next 2 sc on ring, sc in next sc, turn.

PETAL 2
Row 1: Ch 1, sk sc on padding cord, sc in next sc, hdc in each of next 17 dc, 7 hdc over padding cord only, adjust tension of padding cord, turn.

Row 2: Sk first hdc, sc in next hdc, hdc in next hdc, dc in each of next 20 hdc, hdc in next hdc, sc in next sc, sc over padding cord only, sk 2 sc on ring, sc in next sc, turn.

PETALS 3–20
Rows 1 & 2: Rep rows 1 and 2 of Petal 2, join at base of first petal, leaving enough of a tail to sew the first and last petal tog up sides. Fasten off. Weave in ends. Piece will form a cupped shape.

PART C
MAKE 2.
RING
Rnd 1: Work 30 sc over padding cord only, join in first sc of rnd to form ring, adjust padding cord to get size ring desired.

Rnd 2: Working over padding cord throughout piece, ch 1, 2 sc in each st, join in first sc, adjust padding cord tension. *(60 sc)*

PETAL 1

Row 1: Working over padding cord, work sc and 32 hdc, adjust padding cord tension frequently throughout, turn.

Row 2: Sk 1 hdc, sc in next hdc, hdc in next hdc, dc in each of next 28 hdc, hdc in next hdc, sc in next sc, sc over padding cord only, sk 2 sc on ring, sc in next sc, turn.

PETAL 2

Row 1: Ch 1, sk sc on padding cord, sc in next sc, hdc in next hdc, hdc in each of next 25 dc, 6 hdc over padding cord only, adjust tension of padding cord, turn.

Row 2: Sk first hdc, sc in next hdc, hdc in next hdc, dc in each of next 28 hdc, hdc in next hdc, sc in next sc, sc over padding cord only, sk 2 sc on ring, sc in next sc, turn.

PETALS 3–17

Rows 1 & 2: Rep rows 1 and 2 of Petal 2. At the end of Petal 17, fasten off. Weave in ends. *(Petals do not go all the way around the ring; piece will form a cupped shape.)*

PART D CENTER BALL

Rnd 1: Ch 4, join to form ring, ch 1, 8 sc in ring, join in back lp of first sc.

Rnd 2: Working in back lp of entire piece, ch 1, 2 sc in same sc, 2 sc in each st around, join in back lp of first sc. *(16 sc)*

Rnd 3: Ch 1, 2 sc in same sc, sc in next sc, [2 sc in next sc, sc in next sc] around, join in back lp of first sc. *(24 sc)*

Rnd 4: Ch 1, 2 sc in same st, sc in each of next 2 sc, [2 sc in next sc, sc in each of next 2 sc] around, join in back lp of first sc. *(32 sc)*

Rnds 5–11: Ch 1, sc in same sc, sc in each sc around, join in back lp of first sc.

Rnd 12: Sc dec over next 2 sc, sc in each of next 2 sc, [sc dec over next 2 sc, sc in each of next 2 sc] around, join in first sc. *(24 sc)*

Rnd 13: Sc dec over next 2 sc, sc in next sc, [sc dec over next 2 sc, sc in next sc] around, join in first sc. Stuff Ball with fiberfill. *(16 sc)*

Rnds 14 & 15: [Sc dec over next 2 sc] around, join in first sc. At end of rnd 14, fasten off. Weave in end. *(4 sc)*

Sew all pieces tog to create your rose. ■

Chapter 8 FILL-IN LACE

Fill-in lace is used between the motifs on an Irish crochet piece. These samplers give you some idea of the different laces you can use to set your motifs off and make them look their best. Choose simple or more intricate—the choice is yours. Of course, you will have to adjust the laces to fit the areas between your pieces, but having a good idea how each is constructed allows you to make the adjustments more easily.

You can use one style for your whole piece or showcase areas by using different laces in certain places.

1. FILL-IN LACE SAMPLER

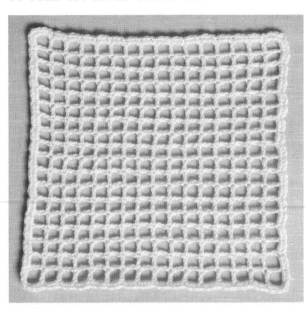

SKILL LEVEL

INTERMEDIATE

FINISHED MEASUREMENT
Sampler: 5½ inches square

MATERIALS

- Size 10 crochet cotton:
  Amount needed varies by piece worked
- Size 7/1.65mm steel crochet hook

Row 1: Ch 53, dc in the 8th ch from hook *(sk chs count as first dc, ch 2, sk 2 foundation chs)*, [ch 2, sk each of next 2 chs, dc in next ch] 15 times, turn. *(16 ch-2 sps)*

Row 2: Ch 5 *(counts as first dc, ch 2)*, dc in next dc, [ch 2, dc in next dc] 15 times, turn.

Rows 3–18: Rep row 2. At the end of row 18, do not turn.

EDGING
Working down side of sampler, (sc, hdc, sc) in next sp, [(sc, hdc, sc) in next ch sp] 16 times, sc in corner sp, (hdc, sc) 3 times in same corner sp, working across bottom edge of sampler, [(sc, hdc, sc) in next ch sp] 14 times, sc in corner sp, (hdc, sc) 3 times in same corner sp, working across side edge of sampler, [(sc, hdc, sc) in next ch sp] 16 times, sc in corner sp, (hdc, sc) 3 times in same corner sp, working across top edge of sampler, [(sc, hdc, sc) in next ch sp] 14 times, (sc, hdc) twice in same corner sp as beg sts, join in first sc. Fasten off. Weave in end. Block.

2. FILL-IN LACE SAMPLER

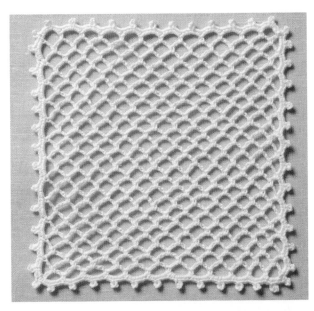

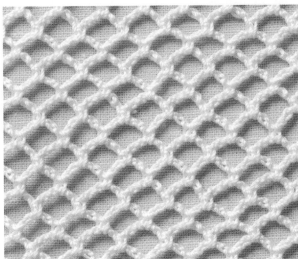

SKILL LEVEL

INTERMEDIATE

FINISHED MEASUREMENT

Sampler: 5½ inches square

MATERIALS

- Size 10 crochet cotton:
  Amount needed varies by piece worked
- Size 7/1.65mm steel crochet hook

Note: *Multiple of 4 + 1 for starting ch.*

Row 1: Ch 55, sc in 10th ch from hook *(sk chs count as turning ch-9 sp)*, [ch 5, sk next 3 chs, sc in next ch] 11 times, turn. *(12 ch sps)*

Row 2: Ch 5, sc in first ch-5 sp, [ch 5, sc in next ch sp] 11 times, ch 2, tr in the 5th ch of ch-9 turning ch to position hook in center of last ch sp, turn.

Row 3: Ch 5, sc in first ch-5 sp, [ch 5, sc in next ch-5 sp] 11 times, turn.

Row 4: Ch 5, sc in first ch-5 sp, [ch 5, sc in next ch-5 sp] 11 times, ch 2, tr in top of tr at end of row before last to position hook in center of last ch sp, turn.

Rows 5–24: [Rep rows 3 and 4 alternately] 10 times.

Row 25: Rep row 3, do not turn.

EDGING

Ch 1, sc in same sc, ch-3 picot in last sc made, [3 sc in next sp, ch-3 picot in last sc made, 2 sc in same sp] 12 times, {sc in next sp, ch-3 picot in last sc made, [3 sc in next sp, ch-3 picot in last sc made, 2 sc in same sp] 12 times} 3 times, join in first sc of rnd. Fasten off. Weave in end. Block.

3. FILL-IN LACE SAMPLER

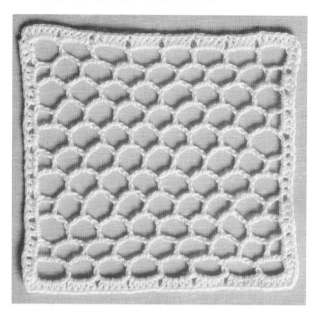

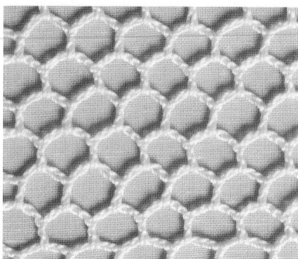

INTERMEDIATE

FINISHED MEASUREMENTS

Sampler: 4½ inches wide x 5¼ inches long

MATERIALS

- Size 10 crochet cotton:
  Amount needed varies by piece
  worked
- Size 7/1.65mm steel crochet hook

Row 1: Ch 56, dc in 14th ch from hook (sk 13 chs count as turning ch), [ch 5, sk next 5 ch sts, dc in next ch st] 7 times, turn.

Row 2: Ch 4, dc in first ch-5 sp, [ch 5, dc in next ch-5 sp] 7 times, ch 2, dc in the 8th ch of turning ch-13 to position hook in center of last ch sp, turn.

Row 3: Ch 7, dc in first ch-5 sp, [ch 5, dc in next ch-5 sp] 6 times, ch 5, dc in the 2nd ch of ch-4 at beg of previous row, turn.

Row 4: Ch 4, dc in first ch-5 sp, [ch 5, dc in next ch-5 sp] 7 times, ch 2, dc in 2nd ch of beg ch-7 of previous row to position hook in center of last ch sp, turn.

Rows 5–10: [Rep rows 3 and 4 alternately] 3 times, turn.

Row 11: Rep row 3, at the end of row 11, turn.

EDGING

Ch 2 (counts as first dc), 2 dc in same st, [5 dc in next ch-5 sp] 8 times, 3 dc in next corner sp, working across side edge of sampler, [2 dc in next ch sp, 3 dc in next ch sp] 5 times, 2 dc in next ch sp, 3 dc in next corner sp, [5 dc in next ch-5 sp] 8 times, 3 dc in next corner sp, working across side edge of sampler [2 dc in next ch sp, 3 dc in next ch sp] 5 times, 2 dc in next ch sp, join in 2nd ch of beg ch-2. Fasten off. Weave in end. Block.

4. FILL-IN LACE SAMPLER

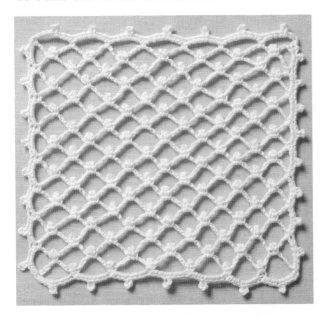

SKILL LEVEL

INTERMEDIATE

FINISHED MEASUREMENTS
Sampler: 5¾ inches wide x 5¼ inches long

MATERIALS

- Size 10 crochet cotton:
  Amount needed varies by piece worked
- Size 7/1.65mm steel crochet hook

Note: *Multiples of 6.*

Row 1: Ch 50, sc in 14th ch from hook (*sk 13 chs count as turning ch*), ch-3 picot in last sc made, sc in same ch, [ch 7, sk next 5 chs, sc in next ch, ch-3 picot in last sc made, sc in same ch] 5 times, ch 7, sk next 5 chs, sc in next ch, turn.

Row 2: Ch 7, sc in next ch-7 sp, ch-3 picot in last sc made, sc in same sp, [ch 7, sc in next ch-7 sp, ch-3 picot in last sc made, sc in same sp] 6 times, ch 3, tr in the 6th ch of ch-13 turning ch to position hook in center of last ch sp, turn.

Row 3: Ch 7, sc in next ch-7 sp, ch-3 picot in last sc made, sc in same sp, [ch 7, sc in next ch-7 sp, ch-3 picot in last sc made, sc in same sp] 5 times, ch 7, sc in next ch-7 sp, turn.

Row 4: Ch 7, sc in next ch-7 sp, ch-3 picot in last sc made, sc in same sp, [ch 7, sc in next ch-7 sp, ch-3 picot in last sc made, sc in same sp] 6 times, ch 3, tr in the top of tr at end of row before last, turn.

Rows 5–16: [Rep rows 3 and 4 alternately] 6 times.

Row 17: Ch 7, sc in next ch-7 sp, [ch 7, sc in next ch-7 sp] 6 times.

EDGING
Working down side of sampler, 3 sc in next sp, ch-3 picot in last sc made, 2 sc in same sp, [(3 sc in next sp, ch-3 picot in last sc made, 2 sc) in same sp] 7 times, working across lower edge, [(4 sc in next ch sp, ch-3 picot in last sc made, 3 sc) in same ch sp] 7 times, working up next side, [(3 sc in next sp, ch-3 picot in last sc made, 2 sc) in same sp] 8 times, working across top edge, [(4 sc in next ch sp, ch-3 picot in last sc made, 3 sc) in same ch sp] 7 times, join in first sc. Fasten off. Weave in end. Block.

5. FILL-IN LACE SAMPLER

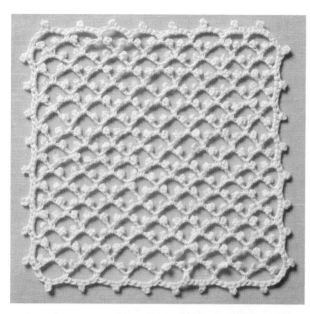

SKILL LEVEL

INTERMEDIATE

FINISHED MEASUREMENTS

Sampler: 6 inches wide x 5⅞ inches long

MATERIALS

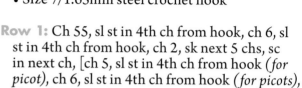

- Size 10 crochet cotton:
  Amount needed varies by piece worked
- Size 7/1.65mm steel crochet hook

Row 1: Ch 55, sl st in 4th ch from hook, ch 6, sl st in 4th ch from hook, ch 2, sk next 5 chs, sc in next ch, [ch 5, sl st in 4th ch from hook *(for picot)*, ch 6, sl st in 4th ch from hook *(for picots)*, ch 2, sk next 5 chs, sc in next ch] 7 times, turn.

Row 2: Ch 9, sl st in 4th ch from hook, ch 2, sc between 2 picots on next ch lp, [ch 5, sl st in 4th ch from hook, ch 6, sl st in 4th ch from hook, ch 2, sc between 2 picots on next ch lp] 7 times, ch 5, sl st in 4th ch from hook, ch 2, tr in the 3rd ch from the first picot on starting ch to position hook in center of last ch sp, turn.

Row 3: Ch 5, sl st in 4th ch from hook, ch 6, sl st in 4th ch from hook, ch 2, sc between 2 picots on next ch lp, [ch 5, sl st in 4th ch from hook, ch 6, sl st in 4th ch from hook, ch 2, sc between 2 picots on next ch lp] 7 times ch 5, sl st in 4th ch from hook, ch 2, tr in 4th ch of ch-9, turn.

Row 4: Ch 9, sl st in 4th ch from hook, ch 2, sc between 2 picots on next ch lp, [ch 5, sl st in 4th ch from hook, ch 6, sl st in 4th ch from hook, ch 2, sc between 2 picots on next ch lp] 7 times, ch 5, sl st in 4th ch from hook, ch 2, tr in top of tr at end of row before last, turn.

Rows 5–16: [Rep rows 3 and 4 alternately] 6 times.

Row 17: Ch 7, dc between 2 picots on next ch lp, [ch 5, dc between 2 picots on next ch lp] 6 times, ch 5, dc in 4th ch of ch-9 at end of row before last.

EDGING

[(3 sc in next sp, ch-3 picot in last sc made, 2 sc) in same sp] around, join in first sc. Fasten off. Weave in end. Block.

6. FILL-IN LACE SAMPLER

Skill Level

INTERMEDIATE

FINISHED MEASUREMENTS
Sampler: 5¼ inches wide x 4¾ inches long

MATERIALS
- Size 10 crochet cotton:
  Amount needed varies by piece worked
- Size 7/1.65mm steel crochet hook

Row 1: Ch 55, sc in 19th ch from hook (*sk 18 chs count as turning ch*), [ch 4, (yo, catch up lp reaching under front of ch st, yo, catch up lp reaching under the back of the ch) 3 times, yo, catch up lp reaching under front of the ch, yo, draw through all lps on hook, sl st in last sc made, gently draw up lp until end of clones knot almost meet (*clones knot made*), sc in same ch st, ch 9, sk next 8 chs, sc in next ch] 4 times, turn.

Row 2: Ch 9, sc in first ch-9 sp, [clones knot, sc in same ch sp, ch 9, sc in next ch-9 sp] 4 times, clones knot, sc in same sp, ch 4, dtr in 9th ch of ch-18 turning ch to position hook in center of ch sp, turn.

Row 3: Ch 9, [sc in next ch-9 sp, clones knot, sc in same sp, ch 9] 4 times, clones knot, sc in same sp, ch 4, ending with sc in next ch-9 sp, turn.

Row 4: Ch 9, sc in first ch-9 sp, [clones knot, sc in same ch st, ch 9, sc in next ch-9 sp] 4 times, clones knot, sc in same sp, ch 4, dtr in top of dtr at end of row before last, turn.

Rows 5–10: [Rep rows 3 and 4 alternately] 3 times.

Row 11: Ch 10, dc in next ch-9 sp, [ch 8, dc in next ch-9 sp] 4 times.

EDGING

Ch 2, 2 dc in same st, working down side of sampler, 3 dc in next ch sp, [7 dc in next ch sp] 5 times, 3 dc in next sc, working across bottom of sampler, [8 dc in next ch-8 sp, dc in bottom of next clones knot] 4 times, 8 dc in next ch-8 sp, 3 dc in next ch, working up the side of sampler, [7 dc in next ch sp] 5 times, 3 dc in next ch-10 sp, 3 dc in 2nd ch of ch-10 sp, 8 dc in same sp, [dc in next dc, 8 dc in next ch-8 sp] 4 times, join in 2nd ch of beg ch-2. Fasten off. Weave in end. Using care not to crush clones knots, block. ∎

Chapter 9
IRISH CROCHET SAMPLER FOR FILL-IN LACE

One of the things that makes Irish crochet special and so beautiful is how it is assembled. By doing separate motifs and then joining them with fill-in lace, it gives the crocheter a much larger license to create beautiful works of art. The only limit is your imagination!

If you want to create a field of flowers as a collar, you have only to create and assemble the motifs you desire, then connect them with your fill-in lace and you have a masterpiece that is truly your own.

There are several ways to do this.

The most traditional way is to make your motifs, and then pin or sew them onto a medium, such as heavy brown paper or a fabric to keep them from shifting from the spot you wish them to be in your creation. Then, working the fill-in lace while the motifs are held in place, adjust your lace to fit the area that is being filled in.

This phase of Irish crochet is not an exact science. There is a lot of trial and error regarding what works for each piece, which is why you will find very few actual patterns for a complete Irish crochet piece.

You will find a lot of patterns for motifs, but complete pieces are almost impossible to write out. All it takes is a motif shifted ¼ inch one way or another, and what worked for one person will not work for another. This is one of the charms of Irish crochet, though—its flexibility. Because we are not limited or restricted by a set pattern, at this point we can adjust our designs to fit our tastes. Irish crochet involves creating a background using the basic technique as a starting point and then working the stitches to fit the spaces created by the motifs within the boundaries of your design.

Another common method is to create a fill-in lace background, and then sew the motifs onto the preworked background in the desired arrangement. This is probably the easiest method, though the look isn't quite the same. However, it does allow a chance to play with the motifs with a little less of a challenge if you feel daunted by the traditional method.

I have included a fairly simple exercise in creating a whole piece from your motifs in this chapter. The border and motifs can be done in either the traditional method or the updated with no pc ring or padding cord. Both methods will be offered in this chapter.

To increase multiple Meshes: Ch 2, edtr in the indicated st *(this is the foundation increase)*, ch 2, edtr in the middle of the edtr st of previous increase, continue in this manner until number of meshes indicated is achieved.

METHOD 1: FILL-IN LACE WORKED AROUND MOTIFS

FINISHED SAMPLER
SAMPLER
Motifs and border patterns given below.

MATERIALS
- Heavy paper or medium-weight fabric
- Sewing thread
- Sewing needle
- Scissors

Note: Paper or fabric needs to be large enough for piece to be sewn to with at least 1-inch border of paper or fabric around piece when sewn in place for easier handling.

Left-Handed

Right-Handed

Pieces needed for Sampler

BORDER FOR IRISH CROCHET ASSEMBLY SAMPLER PC

SKILL LEVEL

INTERMEDIATE

FINISHED MEASUREMENT
6⅛ inches square, blocked

MATERIALS
- Size 10 crochet cotton:
  15 yds white
- Size 7/1.65mm steel crochet hook

Padding cord lengths:

Outside Edging: Cut 2 lengths of white 5 feet long for padding cord, hold tog and fold in half, wrap on padding cord bobbin.

Inside Edging: Cut 2 lengths of white 4 feet long for padding cord, hold tog and fold in half, wrap on padding cord bobbin.

MAIN BODY
Ch 8, edc in 8th ch from hook, ch 2, edtr in the same ch (*that is inc number 1*), {[ch 2, edtr in middle of edtr st of previous inc] 15 times, ch 2,

holding last lp on the hook, edtr in the middle of edtr st of previous inc, yo 6 times, insert hook in middle of the edtr of previous st, yo, draw through 2 lps at a time until all lps are worked off the hook *(corner made)*, ch 2, edtr in the 5th lp worked off 2 lps of corner st} 3 times, [ch 2, edtr in middle of edtr st of previous inc] 15 times, ch 2, making sure nothing is twisted and the piece lays flat, join in top of edc at beg of square, sl st in each of next 3 ch sts, ch 2, again making sure nothing is twisted, sl st in middle of last edtr made. Fasten off. Weave in ends.

OUTSIDE EDGING

Join white in any corner sp, ch 1, sc in same sp and through the fold of the 5-foot padding cord, working over all 4 strands of padding cord around, sc in same sp, ch-3 picot in last sc made, [3 sc in same sp, ch-3 picot in last sc made] twice, sc in same sp, [2 sc in next sp, ch-3 picot in last sc made, sc in same sp] 17 times, *2 sc in next corner sp, ch-3 picot in last sc made, [3 sc in same sp, ch-3 picot in last sc made] twice, sc in same sp, [2 sc in next sp, ch-3 picot in last sc made, sc in same sp] 17 times, rep from * around, ending with join in first sc. Fasten off. Weave in ends.

INNER EDGING

Join white in inside of any corner sp, ch 1, sc in same sp and through fold of 4-foot padding cord, working over all 4 strands of the padding cord around, [3 sc in next sp] 17 times, *sc in next corner sp, [3 sc in next sp] 17 times, rep from * around, ending with join in first sc. Fasten off. Weave in ends.

This could also be done without the padding cord if desired.

MOTIFS
5-PETAL FLOWER & LEAF SPRAY
Note: *This is a 1-way design so your leaves will face 1 direction for a right-handed person and the other direction for a left-handed person.*

5-PETAL FLOWER: TRADITIONAL WITH PC & PR

SKILL LEVEL

INTERMEDIATE

FINISHED MEASUREMENT
2¾ inches across

MATERIALS

- Size 10 crochet cotton:
  30 yds white
- Size 7/1.65mm steel crochet hook
- Size G/6/4mm crochet hook for pc

Padding cord lengths: Cut 2 lengths of white 4 feet long for padding cord, hold tog and fold in half, wrap on padding cord bobbin.

Rnd 1: Using nonworking end of size G hook, make 12-wrap pc ring, 15 sc in ring, join in back lp of first sc.

Rnd 2: Ch 1, *sc in each of next 3 sc, ch 11, sl st in 11th ch from hook, ch 1, working in ch-11 ring just formed (sc, 3 hdc, 4 dc, 3 tr, 4 dc, 3 hdc, sc) in same ring, sl st around base of medallion, rep from * around, ending with join in first sc.

Rnd 3: Sl st in next sc, ch 1, sc in same sc and through fold of padding cord, working over all 4 strands of padding cord threads.

Petal 1: Sk next sc, sc in next sc, sc in each of next 3 hdc, ch-3 picot in last sc made, sc in each of next 3 dc, ch-3 picot in last sc made, sc in next dc, sc in each of next 2 tr, sc in same tr, ch-3 picot in last sc made, sc in same tr, sc in next tr, sc in each of next 2 dc, ch-3 picot in last sc made, sc in each of next 2 dc, sc in next hdc, ch-3 picot in last sc made, sc in each of next 2 hdc, sc in next sc, sk next sc.

Petals 2–4: Sc in next sc, sk next sc, sc in next sc, sc in each of next 3 hdc, ch 1, sl st in last picot on previous petal, ch 1, sl st in last sc made, sc in each of next 3 dc, ch-3 picot in last sc made, sc in next dc, sc in each of next 2 tr, sc in same tr, ch-3 picot in last sc made, sc in same tr, sc in next tr, sc in each of next 2 dc, ch-3 picot in last sc made, sc in each of next 2 dc, sc in next hdc, ch-3 picot in last sc made, sc in each of next 2 hdc, sc in next sc, sk next sc.

Petal 5: Sc in next sc, sk next sc, sc in next sc, sc in each of next 3 hdc, ch 1, sl st in last picot on previous petal, ch 1, sl st in last sc made, sc in each of next 3 dc, ch-3 picot in last sc made, sc in next dc, sc in each of next 2 tr, sc in same tr, ch-3 picot in last sc made, sc in same tr, sc in next tr, sc in each of next 2 dc, ch-3 picot in last sc made, sc in each of next 2 dc, sc in next hdc, ch 1, sl st in first picot on first petal made, ch 1, sl st in last sc made, sc in each of next 2 hdc, sc in next sc, sk next sc, ending with join in first sc. Fasten off. Weave in ends.

LEAF 1
Padding cord lengths: For each leaf, cut 2 lengths of white 12 inches long for padding cord, hold tog and fold in half, wrap on padding cord bobbin.

Rnd 1: Ch 8, sc in 2nd ch from hook, ch 3, sc in same ch, hdc in next ch, dc in next ch, 3 dc in next ch, dc in next ch, hdc in next ch, sc in next ch, ch 3, working in the lp on back side of ch, sc in next ch, hdc in next ch, dc in next ch, 3 dc in next ch, dc in next ch, hdc in next ch, ending with join in first sc.

Rnd 2: Ch 1, sc in same sc and through fold of padding cord, working over all 4 strands of padding cord around, 2 sc in next ch-3 sp, ch 5, sl st in top of last sc made (*ch-5 picot made*), sc in same sp, sc in next sc, sc in next hdc, ch 3, sl st in top of last sc made (*ch-3 picot made*), sc in each of next 3 dc, ch-3 picot in last sc made, sc in each of next 2 dc, sc in next hdc, ch-3 picot in last sc made, sc in next sc, 2 sc in next ch-3 sp, ch 14, sc in picot joining between any petal on flower, turn, sc in 14th ch st, sc in each of rem chs, sc in same sp, sc in next sc, sc in next hdc, ch-3 picot in last sc made, sc in each of next 3 dc, ch-3 picot in last sc made, sc in each of next 2 dc, sc in next hdc, ch-3 picot in last sc made, ending with join in first sc of rnd. Fasten off. Weave in ends.

LEAF 2
Rnd 1: Rep rnd 1 of Leaf 1.

Rnd 2: Ch 1, sc in same sc and through fold of padding cord, working over all 4 strands of padding cord around, 2 sc in next ch-3 sp, ch 5 picot in last sc made, sc in same sp, sc in next sc, sc in next hdc, ch-3 picot in last sc made, sc in each of next 3 dc, ch-3 picot in last sc made, sc in each of next 2 dc, sc in next hdc, ch-3 picot in last sc made, sc in next sc, 2 sc in next ch-3 sp, ch 8, sl st in 5th sc on stem from Leaf 1, sl st in next sc on stem, turn, sc in 8th ch st, sc in each of next 7 chs, sc in same sp, sc in next sc, sc in next hdc, ch-3 picot in last sc made, sc in each of next 3 dc, ch-3 picot in last sc made, sc in each of next 2 dc, sc in next hdc, ch-3 picot in last sc made, ending with join in first sc. Fasten off. Weave in ends.

LEAF 3
Rnd 1: Rep rnd 1 of Leaf 1.

Rnd 2: Ch 1, sc in same sc and through fold of padding cord, working over all 4 strands of padding cord around, 2 sc in next ch-3 sp, ch 5 picot in last sc made, sc in same sp, sc in next sc, sc in next hdc, ch-3 picot in last sc made, sc in each of next 3 dc, ch-3 picot in last sc made, sc in each of next 2 dc, sc in next hdc, ch-3 picot in last sc made, sc in next sc, 2 sc in next ch-3 sp, ch 8, sl st in 4th free ch lp on opposite side of foundation ch of stem nearest the flower, sl st in next free ch lp on stem, turn, sc in 8th ch, sc in each of next 7 chs, sc in same sp, sc in next sc, sc in next hdc, ch-3 picot in last sc made, sc in each of next 3 dc, ch-3 picot in last sc made, sc in each of next 2 dc, sc in next hdc, ch-3 picot in last sc made, ending with join in first sc. Fasten off. Weave in ends.

RING WITH PICOTS 8 POINTS

SKILL LEVEL

EASY

FINISHED MEASUREMENT

¾ inch across

MATERIALS

- Size 10 crochet cotton:
  2 yds white
- Size 7/1.65mm steel crochet hook
- Size G/6/4mm crochet hook for pc

Using nonworking end of size G hook, with white, make 12-wrap pc ring, sc in ring, ch 3, (2 sc in ring, ch 3) 7 times, sc in ring, join in first sc. Fasten off. Weave in end.

6-PETAL ROSE WITH PICOTS PR

SKILL LEVEL

INTERMEDIATE

FINISHED MEASUREMENT

1¼ inches across

MATERIALS

- Size 10 crochet cotton:
  10 yds white
- Size 7/1.65mm steel crochet hook
- Size G/6/4mm crochet hook for pc

Rnd 1: Using nonworking end of size G hook, with white, make 12-wrap pc ring, 12 sc in ring, join in first sc (*traditional*); or, ch 5, join to form ring (*updated*), 12 sc in ring, join in first sc.

Rnd 2: Ch 1, sc in same sc, ch 3, sk next sc, [sc in next sc, ch 3, sk next sc] around, join in first sc. (*6 ch-3 lps*)

Rnd 3: Sl st in ch-3 lp, ch 1, [(sc, 3 dc, ch-3 picot in last dc made, 2 dc, sc) all in the same ch-3 lp] around, join in first sc. Fasten off. Weave in end. (*6 petals*)

ASSEMBLY

Once all your motifs are completed, decide how you want to arrange your pieces. The sampler motifs given can be varied to suit your taste. I am teaching a method here and do not expect anyone to copy it exactly. Your piece should be fairly close if desired, but it will still be your piece; there is going to be variation.

But that is part of what Irish crochet is all about.

Block your motifs and edging at this point. Do not use any starch at this point when blocking. You just want the pieces to be the size and shape you desire when finished. Starching them at this point will make it harder to work in the sts.

MOTIFS & BORDER BASTED ON FABRIC

After you have decided how you want things placed within your border, you will baste the pieces onto your fabric or paper. You can sew them either right sides facing the fabric or you can sew them with the right sides facing up toward you. Either way is correct and a matter of personal preference. The only rule is: Be consistent. If you do right side facing the fabric, all the motifs and the border should face the same way.

I like to use a contrasting thread for basting my piece down. This will make it easier to see and remove when the piece is done.

When basting down the pieces, the main concern should be that they don't shift around while you are working your fill-in lace. You don't need to take tiny stitches, but you also shouldn't use such large stitches that the motifs are liable to shift while you crochet your fill-in lace. Do not pull the sewing thread so tight that it bunches up your backing material. You want your pieces to be on a nice smooth surface at this point. No ripples or puckers to distort the final piece.

After the pieces have all been basted onto your fabric, then you can begin your fill-in lace. If you have a lot of open spaces on your piece, decide which are the top and the bottom so you can work your fill-in lace the direction you desire for the larger areas where you are using just the fill-in lace to create part of the design.

Starting at a lower corner, attach your thread so you will be working across the bottom edge of your piece. In this case, I started on the bottom left-hand corner since I am left-handed. A right-handed person would start most likely in the right-hand corner.

The first row of the sample was ch-5s, skipping 4 sc on inner edge and sc in next sc, rep across bottom. Do not worry if this will fit your space exactly. Fill-in lace is not about the numbers, but about the look. Even if I could do that on this piece, I purposefully won't, as I intend to show you how to use this technique on any Irish crochet design you wish to do. You can adjust how many sts you chain or how many you skip to suit the look you want.

WORK IN PROGRESS

METHOD OF ATTACHING TO A MOTIF MIDDLE OF CH SP

Ch number of chs to comfortably reach motif or edging, sl st or sc to the point at which you wish to attach your fill-in lace on a motif or edging, continue with chs to comfortably reach next ch sp, or edging, sc in ch sp or edging as desired.

METHODS OF ATTACHING TO A SINGLE POINT

Besides just chaining and joining with sc or sl st in desired st, there will be times when you don't want your next ch sp to start where the ch would leave your work.

At this time you can use ch 2 or 3 (this will depend on where you need to reach and how you want the ch sp to lay), leaving the last lp of each st on the hook, work dc or tr (depending on length of st needed to reach the place you wish to fill in), sk however many sts needed to place the st where desired, yo, draw through all lps on hook, you can move on from there or turn depending on where you need to go for your next ch sp.

METHODS OF ATTACHING TO MULTIPLE POINTS (2-POINT)

Ch 2 or 3 (*this will depend on where you need to reach and how you want the ch sp to lay*), leaving the last lp of each st on the hook, work a dc or tr (*depending on length of st needed to reach the place you wish to fill in*), sk the number of sts needed to place the st where desired, dc or tr (*depending again on the length of the st needed to reach the place you wish to fill in*) in the next place that you wish to attach your fill-in lace (*on the side, in a motif or in another ch sp*), yo, draw through all lps on hook, you can move on from there or turn depending on where you need to go for your next ch sp.

Note: *Never feel limited by the number of chs or the size of the st you use. If more ch sts work better or if a dtr works best, by all means use it.*

You will find yourself working in a small area of your design at times, compared to the whole design, working back and forth in that area to fill it in. You will rarely work in just rows across your whole piece or you will be ending off too often. Normally you will work in rows when you have larger areas of open spaces to fill in.

You will find yourself working sideways, even upside down at times to make the ch sps fit the area you need and want to fill in. Sometimes you will work yourself into an area that you will have to end off and reattach in a different area; this is normal.

I did warn you this is not an exact science!

Always check your work often to make sure the piece is still lying flat. If the fabric begins to buckle or bunch, you have worked your fill-in lace too tight and you need to redo the section that is creating the pull. I normally check after about 3 ch sps have been completed to see how it looks and how it is lying.

Keep working in this manner until you have filled in your entire piece. Always take a look at how the fill-in lace affects the look of your piece as you go. It's easier to make small adjustments as you work than to remove sections once they have been done and start over.

Once the piece is filled in to your satisfaction, then you can remove the piece from the fabric.

Cut and pull the basting threads from the back side of the fabric. This will lessen the chance that you will accidentally snip one of the threads on your masterpiece.

Check your piece over once you remove it from the fabric to make sure all the sewing thread has been removed.

You can block again if you so desire.

This sampler was done with simple ch sps for the fill-in lace. Once you understand how to do the technique, you can then start using any of the other fill-in laces you desire.

METHOD 2: MOTIFS SEWN ON

BACKGROUND OF FILL-IN LACE SAMPLER

SKILL LEVEL

INTERMEDIATE

FINISHED MEASUREMENT

6⅛ inches square, blocked

MATERIALS

- Motifs used for Sampler for Method 1
- Size 10 crochet cotton:
   Amount needed varies by piece worked
- Size 7/1.65mm steel crochet hook
- Sewing thread to match motifs
- Sewing needle
- Straight pins
- Scissors

BACKGROUND FOR SAMPLER

Row 1: Ch 54, sc in 10th ch from hook, [ch 5, sk each of next 3 chs, sc in next ch] 11 times, turn.

Row 2: Ch 5, sc in first ch-5 sp, [ch 5, sc in next ch-5 sp] 11 times, ch 2, tr in the 4th ch of ch-9 turning ch to position hook in center of last ch sp, turn.

Row 3: Ch 5, sc in first ch-5 sp, [ch 5, sc in next ch-5 sp] 11 times, turn.

Row 4: Ch 5, sc in first ch-5 sp, [ch 5, sc in next ch-5 sp] 11 times, ch 2, tr in top of tr from row before last row to position hook in center of last ch sp, turn.

Rows 5–24: [Rep rows 3 and 4 alternately] 10 times.

Row 25: Rep row 3.

EDGING

Ch 1, sc in first sc, ch-3 picot in last sc made, [3 sc in next sp, ch-3 picot in last sc made, 2 sc in same sp] 12 times, {sc in next sc or corner ch, ch-3 picot in last sc made, [3 sc in next sp, ch-3 picot in last sc made, 2 sc in same sp] 12 times} 3 times, ending with join in first sc. Fasten off. Weave in ends. Block.

ASSEMBLY

Arrange your blocked motif pieces on your background as desired. Pin in place so they will not shift while sewing in place. Using matching sewing thread, sew all your motifs onto background, taking care that sts don't show. ∎

Chapter 10 SQUARES & MOTIFS

Irish crochet techniques can also be used to make squares or motifs that join together. These squares can all be done individually and joined together to make a larger piece without fill-in lace. These can be used to make bedspreads, tablecloths, runners, shawls or whatever you can envision. Let your imagination flow and use these motifs in any way you desire.

1. MESH SQUARE PC

SKILL LEVEL

INTERMEDIATE

FINISHED MEASUREMENT

3¼ inches square

MATERIALS

- Size 10 crochet cotton:
  20 yds white
- Size 7/1.65mm steel crochet hook

Padding cord lengths: [Cut 2 lengths of white 1 yd long for padding cord, hold tog and fold in half, wrap on padding cord bobbin] twice.

Row 1: Ch 23, edc in 8th ch from hook, [ch 2, sk next 2 chs, edc in next ch] 5 times, turn.

Rows 2–6: Ch 5, edc in next edc, [ch 2, edc in next edc] 4 times, ch 2, sk next 2 chs, edc in next ch, turn.

Rnd 1: Now working in rnds, ch 1, sc in same sp and through fold of padding cord, working over all 4 strands of the padding cord around, 3 sc in same sp, [3 sc in next sp] 4 times, *7 sc in next corner sp, [3 sc in next sp] 4 times, rep from * around, ending with 3 sc in first corner sp, join in first sc, drop padding cord, fasten off padding cord. Weave in ends.

Rnd 2: Ch 3, holding last lp of each st on hook, 2 dtr in same st, yo, draw through all lps on hook (*beg 3-dtr cl*), (ch 4, 3-dtr cl in same st) 4 times, ch 4, sk next 8 sc, sc in each of next 2 sc, ch 4, sk next 8 sc, *3-dtr cl in next sc, (ch 4, 3-dtr cl in same st) 4 times, ch 4, sk next 8 sc, sc in each of next 2 sc, ch 4, sk next 8 sc, rep from * around, ending with join in top of beg cl and through fold of next prepared padding cord.

Rnd 3: Ch 1, working over all 4 strands of padding cord around, *[(3 sc, ch 3, 3 sc) in next ch-4 sp] 4 times, (3 sc, ch 3, 2 sc) in next ch-4 sp, sc in next sc, ch 3, sc in next sc, (2 sc, ch 3, 3 sc) in next ch-4 sp, rep from * around, ending with join in first sc. Fasten off. Weave in ends.

2. SQUARE PR

SKILL LEVEL

■■■□
INTERMEDIATE

FINISHED MEASUREMENT
3¾ inches square

MATERIALS
- Size 10 crochet cotton:
  25 yds white
- Size 7/1.65mm steel crochet hook
- Size H/8/5mm crochet hook for pc

0 LACE

Rnd 1: Using the nonworking end of size H hook, with white, make a 12-wrap pc ring, 5 sc in ring, ch 8, (6 sc in ring, ch 8) 3 times, sc in ring, join in first sc.

Rnd 2: Ch 1, sc in same st, sc in each of next 3 sc, sk next sc, 4 sc in next ch-8 sp, (ch 3, sc in same ch-8 sp) 5 times, 3 sc in same ch-8 sp, *sk next sc, sc in each of next 4 sc, sk next sc, 4 sc in next ch-8 sp, (ch 3, sc in same ch-8 sp) 5 times, 3 sc

in same ch-8 sp, rep from * around, join in first sc. Fasten off. Weave in end.

Rnd 3: Join white in the first ch-3 sp on any point, ch 1, sc in same sp, ch 5, sk next ch-3 sp, (sc, ch 7, sc) in next ch-3 sp, ch 5, sk next ch-3 sp, sc in next ch-3 sp, ch 3, *sc in next ch-3 sp on next point, ch 5, sk next ch-3 sp, (sc, ch 7, sc) in next ch-3 sp, ch 5, sk next ch-3 sp, sc in next ch-3 sp, ch 3, rep from * around, join in first sc.

Rnd 4: Sl st in next ch-5 sp, ch 1, 2 sc in same ch-5 sp, *(ch 3, 2 sc in same ch-5 sp) twice, 2 sc in next ch-7 sp, (ch 3, 2 sc in same ch-7 sp) 3 times, 2 sc in next ch-5 sp, (ch 3, 2 sc in same ch-5 sp) twice, (2 sc, ch 3, 2 sc) in next ch-3 sp**, 2 sc in next ch-5 sp, rep from * around, ending last rep at **, join in first sc. Fasten off. Weave in ends.

Rnd 5: Join white in center ch-3 sp on any corner point, ch 7 *(counts as first dc, ch 5)*, dc in same ch-3 sp, *ch 5, sk next ch-3 sp, dc in next ch-3 sp, ch 5, sk next ch-3 sp, tr in next ch-3 sp, ch 5, sk next ch-3 sp, dc in next ch-3 sp, ch 5, sk next ch 3 sp**, (dc, ch 5, dc) in next ch-3 sp at corner point, rep from * around, ending last rep at **, join in 2nd ch of beg ch-7.

Rnd 6: Sl st in next ch-5 sp, ch 1, 8 sc in same ch-5 sp, *ch 3, turn, sk first 3 sc, (dc, ch 3, dc) in next sc, ch 3, sk next 2 sc, sc in next sc, sl st in next sc, ch 1, turn, [(3 sc, ch-3 picot in last sc made, 2 sc) in next ch-3 sp] 3 times, sc in same ch-5 sp, (3 sc, ch-3 picot in last sc made, 2 sc) in next ch-5 sp, 5 sc in next ch 5 sp, sc in next tr, 4 sc in next ch 5 sp, ch 3 turn, (dc, ch 3, dc) in sc worked in tr, ch 3, sk next 3 sc, sc in next sc, sl st in next sc, ch 1, turn, [(3 sc, ch-3 picot in last sc made, 2 sc) in next ch 3 sp] 3 times, sc in same ch-5 sp, (3 sc, ch-3 picot in last sc made, 2 sc) in next ch-5 sp**, 8 sc in next ch-5 sp, rep from * around, ending last rep at **, join in first sc. Fasten off. Weave in end.

3. ROSE & LEAVES MOTIF

SKILL LEVEL

INTERMEDIATE

FINISHED MEASUREMENT

6 inches across

MATERIALS

- Size 10 crochet cotton:
  35 yds white
- Size 7/1.65mm steel crochet hook
- Size G/6/4mm crochet hook for pc

0 LACE

Rnd 1: Using nonworking end of size G hook, with white, make 12-wrap pc ring, 12 sc in ring, join in first sc (*traditional*); or, ch 5, join to form a ring (*updated*), 12 sc in ring, join in first sc.

Rnd 2: Ch 1, sc in same sc, ch 3, sk next sc, [sc in next sc, ch 3, sk next sc] around, join in first sc. (*6 ch-3 lps*)

Rnd 3: Sl st in ch-3 lp, ch 1, (sc, 5 dc, sc) in each ch-3 lp around, join in first sc. (*6 petals*)

Rnd 4: Ch 1, working behind petals on previous rnd, sc around first sc of rnd 2, ch 4, [sc around next sc of rnd 2, ch 4] around, join in first sc. (*6 ch 4-lps*)

Rnd 5: Sl st in ch-4 lp, ch 1, (sc, 7 dc, sc) in each ch-4 lp around, join in first sc. (*6 petals*)

Rnd 6: Ch 1, working behind petals on previous rnd, sc around first sc of rnd 4, ch 5, [sc around next sc of rnd 4, ch 5] around, join in first sc. (*6 ch 5-lps*)

Rnd 7: Sl st in ch-5 lp, ch 1, (sc, 9 dc, sc) in each ch-5 lp around, join in first sc. Fasten off. Weave in end. (*6 petals*)

Leaf 1: Ch 8, sc in 3rd ch from hook, sc in each rem ch across, ch 3, sc in each of next 5 chs on opposite side of foundation ch, ch 2, turn, sc in 2nd ch from hook, working in back lp, sc in each of next 5 sc, (sc, ch 3, sc) in ch-3 lp, working up opposite side of leaf in back lp, sc in each of next 5 sc, *ch 2, turn, sc in 2nd ch from hook, working in back lp, sc in each of next 6 sc, (sc, ch 3, sc) in ch-3 lp, working up opposite side of leaf in back lp, sc in each of next 5 sc, rep from * until you have 1 center point and 5 side points on 1 side and are up to the ch 2 on 5th point on last side, ch 2, turn, sc in 2nd ch from hook, working in back lp, sc in each of next 6 sc, 2 sc in ch-3 lp, working on back side of rose, sl st around any sc of rnd 6 of rose, sc in same lp, sl st into next sc. Fasten off. Weave in ends.

Leaf 2–5: Rep Leaf 1 until you have 1 center point and 5 side points on 1 side and are up to ch 2 on 5th point on last side, ch 2, sl st in point on previous leaf closest to the flower, turn, sc in 2nd ch from hook, working in back lp, sc in each of next 6 sc, 2 sc in ch-3 lp, working on back side of rose, sl st around next sc of rnd 6 of Rose, sc in same lp, sl st in next sc. Fasten off. Weave in ends.

Leaf 6: Rep Leaf 1 until you have one center point and 4 side points on 1 side and are up to ch 2 on 5th point on first side, ch 1, sl st in the point closest to the flower on the first leaf, turn, working in back lp, sc in each of next 6 sc, (sc, ch 3, sc) in next ch-3 lp, sc in each of next 5 sc, ch 2, sl st in point on previous leaf closest to the flower, turn sc in 2nd ch from hook, working in back lp only, sc in each of next 6 sc, 2 sc in ch-3 lp, working on back side of rose, sl st around next sc of rnd 6 of rose, sc in same lp, sl st in next sc. Fasten off. Weave in ends.

4. ROSE & PICOT SQUARE

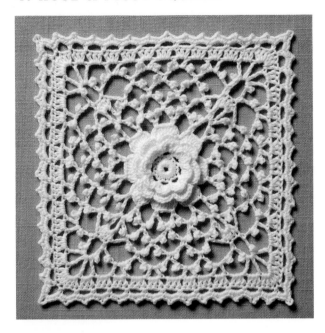

SKILL LEVEL

◼◼◼◻
INTERMEDIATE

FINISHED MEASUREMENT

5¼ inches square

MATERIALS

- Size 10 crochet cotton:
  35 yds white
- Size 7/1.65mm steel crochet hook
- Size G/6/4mm crochet hook for pc

[0] LACE

Rnd 1: Using nonworking end of size G hook, with white, make 12-wrap pc ring, 16 sc in ring, join in first sc *(traditional)*; or, ch 5, join to form a ring *(updated)*, 16 sc in ring, join in first sc.

Rnd 2: Ch 1, sc in same sc, ch 3, sk next sc, [sc in next sc, ch 3, sk next sc] around, join in first sc. *(8 ch-3 lps)*

Rnd 3: Sl st in ch-3 lp, ch 1, (sc, 5 dc, sc) in each ch-3 lp around, join in first sc. *(8 petals)*

Rnd 4: Ch 1, working behind petals on previous rnd, sc around first sc of rnd 2, ch 4, [sc around next sc of rnd 2, ch 4] around, join in first sc. *(8 ch 4-lps)*

Rnd 5: Sl st in ch-4 lp, ch 1, (sc, 7 dc, sc) in each ch-4 lp around, join in first sc. *(8 petals)*

Rnd 6: Ch 1, working behind petals on previous rnd, sc around first sc of rnd 4, ch 5, [sc around next sc of rnd 4, ch 5] around, join in first sc. *(8 ch 5-lps)*

Rnd 7: Sl st in ch-5 lp, ch 1, (sc, 9 dc, sc) in each ch-5 lp around, join in first sc. *(8 petals)*

Rnd 8: Sl st in 3rd dc on next petal, ch 1, sc in same st, ch 5, sl st in 4th ch from hook for picot, ch 6, sl st in 4th ch from hook for picot, ch 2, sk next 3 dc, sc in next dc, ch 5, sl st in 4th ch from hook for picot, ch 6, sl st in 4th ch from hook for picot, ch 2, *sc in 3rd dc on next petal, ch 5, sl st in 4th ch from hook for picot, ch 6, sl st in 4th ch from hook for picot, ch 2, sk next 3 dc, sc in next dc, ch 5, sl st in 4th ch from hook for picot, ch 6, sl st in 4th ch from hook for picot, ch 2, rep from * around, ending with join in first sc.

Rnd 9: Sl st in the ch sp between the next 2 picots, ch 1, sc in same sp, *ch 7, sc in same sp, [ch 5, sl st in 4th ch from hook for picot, ch 6, sl st in 4th ch from hook for picot, ch 2, sk next 2 picots**, sc in next ch-3 sp] 4 times, rep from * around, ending last rep at**, join in first sc.

Rnd 10: Sl st in ch-7 sp, ch 2 *(counts as first dc)*, 4 dc in same sp, *ch 3, sk next picot, sc in next ch-3 sp, [ch 5, sl st in 4th ch from hook for picot, ch 6, sl st in 4th ch from hook for picot, ch 2, sk next 2 picots, sc in next ch-3 sp] 3 times, ch 3**, 5 dc in next ch-7 sp, rep from * around, ending last rep at **, join in 2nd ch of beg ch-2.

Rnd 11: Sl st in next dc, ch 1, sc in same st, ch 5, sl st in 4th ch from hook for picot, ch 6, sl st in 4th ch from hook for picot, ch 2, sk next dc, sc in next dc, [ch 5, sl st in 4th ch from hook for picot, ch 6, sl st in 4th ch from hook for picot, ch 2, sk next 2 picots, sc in next ch-3 sp] 3 times, *[ch 5, sl st in 4th ch from hook, ch 6, sl st in 4th ch from hook, ch 2, sk next dc, sc in next dc] twice [ch 5, sl st in 4th ch from hook for picot, ch 6, sl st in 4th ch from hook, ch 2, sk next 2 picots, sc in next ch-3 sp] 3 times, rep from * around, ending with ch 5, sl st in 4th ch from hook for picot, ch 6, sl st in 4th ch from hook for picot, ch 2, sk next dc, join in first sc at beg of rnd.

Rnd 12: Sl st in next ch-3 sp between picots, ch 4 *(counts as first dc, ch 2)*, tr in same sp, ch 3, tr in same sp, ch 2, tr in same sp, [ch 3, sk next 2 picots, (dc, ch 2, dc) in next ch-3 sp] 4 times, ch 3, sk next 2 picots, *tr in next ch-3 sp, ch 2, tr in same sp, ch 3, tr in same sp, ch 2, tr in same sp, [ch 3, sk next 2 picots, (dc, ch 2, dc) in next ch-3 sp] 4 times, ch 3, sk next 2 picots, rep from * around, ending with join in 2nd ch of beg ch-4.

Rnd 13: Sl st in ch-2 sp, ch 2, 2 dc in same sp, 7 dc in corner ch-3 sp, [3 dc in next ch-2 sp, 3 dc in next ch-3 sp] 5 times, *3 dc in next ch-2 sp, 7 dc in next ch-3 sp, [3 dc in next ch-2 sp, 3 dc in next ch-3 sp] 5 times, rep from * around, join in beg ch-2.

Rnd 14: Ch 1, sc in same sp, [ch 3, sk next 2 dc, sc in next dc] twice, {ch 5, sc in next dc, [ch 3, sk next 2 dc, sc in next dc] 13 times} 3 times, ch 5, sc in next dc, [ch 3, sk next 2 dc, sc in next dc] 10 times, ch 5, join in first sc.

Rnd 15: Sl st into next ch-3 sp, ch 1, (2 sc, ch 2, 2 sc) in same ch-3 sp, (2 sc, ch 2, 2 sc) in next ch-3 sp, {(3 sc, ch 3, 3 sc) in next corner ch-5 sp, [(2 sc, ch 2, 2 sc) in next ch-3 sp] 13 times} 3 times, (3 sc, ch 3, 3 sc) in next corner ch-5 sp, [(2 sc, ch 2, 2 sc) in next ch-3 sp] 11 times, join in first sc. Fasten off. Weave in ends.

5. DAISY WHEEL MOTIF PC & PR

SKILL LEVEL

INTERMEDIATE

FINISHED MEASUREMENT
5 inches across

MATERIALS
- Size 10 crochet cotton: 30 yds white
- Size 7/1.65mm steel crochet hook
- Size G/6/4mm crochet hook for pc

Padding cord lengths: Cut 2 lengths of white each 5 feet long for padding cord, hold tog and fold in half, wrap on padding cord bobbin.

Rnd 1: Using nonworking end of size G hook, with white, make 12-wrap pc ring, 12 sc in ring, join in first sc.

Petal 1: Ch 1, sc in same sc and through fold of padding cord, working over all 4 strands of padding cord around unless otherwise noted, 8 sc worked over padding cord only, ch 1, turn, sc in next 8 sc and over padding cord (*adjust padding cord frequently on this motif*), sc in next sc on ring, turn.

Petals 2–12: [Sc in each of next 5 sc, work 3 sc over padding cord only, ch 1, turn, sc in each of next 8 sc and over padding cord, sc in next sc on ring, turn] 11 times. Leaving 6-inch length, fasten off. Using rem length, sew first and last petals tog across 5 sts. Weave padding cords and ends in.

Rnd 2: Join thread in tip of any petal, ch 1, sc in same st, [ch 5, sl st in 4th ch from hook for picot, ch 6, sl st in 4th ch from hook for picot, ch 2, sc in tip of next petal] 11 times, ch 5, sl st in the 4th ch from hook for picot, ch 6, sl st in 4th ch from hook for picot, ch 2, join in first sc.

Rnd 3: Sl st in center of ch sp between 2 picots, ch 1, sc in same sp, [ch 6, sl st in 4th ch from hook for picot, ch 7, sl st in 4th ch from hook for picot, ch 3, sk next 2 picots, sc in next ch sp] 11 times, ch 6, sl st in 4th ch from hook for picot, ch 7, sl st in 4th ch from hook for picot, ch 3, join in first sc.

Rnd 4: Sl st in center of ch sp between 2 picots, ch 7 (*counts as first dc, ch 5*), dc in same sp, [ch 5, sk next 2 picots, (dc, ch 5, dc) in next ch sp] around, ending with ch 2, edc in 2nd ch of beg ch-7 to position hook in center of last ch sp.

Rnd 5: Ch 1, 3 sc in same sp, 5 sc in next ch-5 sp, 2 sc in next ch-5 sp, ch 3, turn, sk next 3 sc, (dc, ch 3, dc) in center sc of 5-sc group, ch 3, sk next 3 sc, sc in next sc, sl st in next sc, ch 1, turn, [(3 sc, ch-3 picot, 2 sc) in next ch-3 sp] 3 times, *3 sc in same ch-5 sp, 5 sc in next ch-5 sp, 2 sc in next ch-5 sp, ch 3, turn, sk next 3 sc, (dc, ch 3, dc) in center sc of 5-sc group, ch 3, sk next 3 sc, sc in next sc, sl st in next sc, ch 1, turn, [(3 sc, ch-3 picot, 2 sc) in next ch-3 sp] 3 times, rep from * around, ending with join in first sc. Fasten off. Weave in ends.

It is my hope that you find the motifs in this book useful in your Irish crochet creations. It gives me great joy to know that these motifs will be used and appreciated in a new manner. ∎

Notes

STITCH GUIDE

STITCH ABBREVIATIONS

beg	begin/begins/beginning
bpdc	back post double crochet
bpsc	back post single crochet
bptr	back post treble crochet
CC	contrasting color
ch(s)	chain(s)
ch-	refers to chain or space previously made (i.e., ch-1 space)
ch sp(s)	chain space(s)
cl(s)	cluster(s)
cm	centimeter(s)
dc	double crochet (singular/plural)
dc dec	double crochet 2 or more stitches together, as indicated
dec	decrease/decreases/decreasing
dtr	double treble crochet
ext	extended
fpdc	front post double crochet
fpsc	front post single crochet
fptr	front post treble crochet
g	gram(s)
hdc	half double crochet
hdc dec	half double crochet 2 or more stitches together, as indicated
inc	increase/increases/increasing
lp(s)	loop(s)
MC	main color
mm	millimeter(s)
oz	ounce(s)
pc	popcorn(s)
rem	remain/remains/remaining
rep(s)	repeat(s)
rnd(s)	round(s)
RS	right side
sc	single crochet (singular/plural)
sc dec	single crochet 2 or more stitches together, as indicated
sk	skip/skipped/skipping
sl st(s)	slip stitch(es)
sp(s)	space(s)/spaced
st(s)	stitch(es)
tog	together
tr	treble crochet
trtr	triple treble
WS	wrong side
yd(s)	yard(s)
yo	yarn over

YARN CONVERSION

OUNCES TO GRAMS		GRAMS TO OUNCES	
1	28.4	25	⅞
2	56.7	40	1⅔
3	85.0	50	1¾
4	113.4	100	3½

UNITED STATES		UNITED KINGDOM
sl st (slip stitch)	=	sc (single crochet)
sc (single crochet)	=	dc (double crochet)
hdc (half double crochet)	=	htr (half treble crochet)
dc (double crochet)	=	tr (treble crochet)
tr (treble crochet)	=	dtr (double treble crochet)
dtr (double treble crochet)	=	ttr (triple treble crochet)
skip	=	miss

Reverse single crochet (reverse sc): Ch 1, sk first st, working from left to right, insert hook in next st from front to back, draw up lp on hook, yo and draw through both lps on hook.

Chain (ch): Yo, pull through lp on hook.

Single crochet (sc): Insert hook in st, yo, pull through st, yo, pull through both lps on hook.

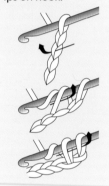

Double crochet (dc): Yo, insert hook in st, yo, pull through st, [yo, pull through 2 lps] twice.

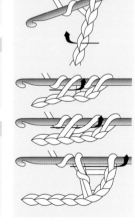

Front loop (front lp) Back loop (back lp)

Front Loop   Back Loop

Front post stitch (fp): Back post stitch (bp): When working post st, insert hook from right to left around post of st on previous row.

Back   Front

Post of Stitch

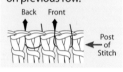

Half double crochet (hdc): Yo, insert hook in st, yo, pull through st, yo, pull through all 3 lps on hook.

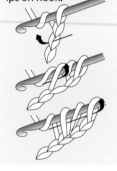

Double treble crochet (dtr): Yo 3 times, insert hook in st, yo, pull through st, [yo, pull through 2 lps] 4 times.

Slip stitch (sl st): Insert hook in st, pull through both lps on hook.

Chain color change (ch color change) Yo with new color, draw through last lp on hook.

Double crochet color change (dc color change) Drop first color, yo with new color, draw through last 2 lps of st.

Treble crochet (tr): Yo twice, insert hook in st, yo, pull through st, [yo, pull through 2 lps] 3 times.

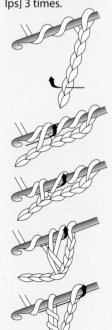

Single crochet decrease (sc dec): (Insert hook, yo, draw lp through) in each of the sts indicated, yo, draw through all lps on hook.

Example of 2-sc dec

Half double crochet decrease (hdc dec): (Yo, insert hook, yo, draw lp through) in each of the sts indicated, yo, draw through all lps on hook.

Example of 2-hdc dec

Double crochet decrease (dc dec): (Yo, insert hook, yo, draw lp through, yo, draw through 2 lps on hook) in each of the sts indicated, yo, draw through all lps on hook.

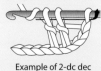

Example of 2-dc dec

Treble crochet decrease (tr dec): Holding back last lp of each st, tr in each of the sts indicated, yo, pull through all lps on hook.

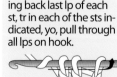

Example of 2-tr dec

Metric Conversion Charts

METRIC CONVERSIONS

yards	x	.9144	= metres (m)
yards	x	91.44	= centimetres (cm)
inches	x	2.54	= centimetres (cm)
inches	x	25.40	= millimetres (mm)
inches	x	.0254	= metres (m)

centimetres	x	.3937	= inches
metres	x	1.0936	= yards

INCHES INTO MILLIMETRES & CENTIMETRES (Rounded off slightly)

inches	mm	cm	inches	cm	inches	cm	inches	cm
1/8	3	0.3	5	12.5	21	53.5	38	96.5
1/4	6	0.6	5 1/2	14	22	56	39	99
3/8	10	1	6	15	23	58.5	40	101.5
1/2	13	1.3	7	18	24	61	41	104
5/8	15	1.5	8	20.5	25	63.5	42	106.5
3/4	20	2	9	23	26	66	43	109
7/8	22	2.2	10	25.5	27	68.5	44	112
1	25	2.5	11	28	28	71	45	114.5
1 1/4	32	3.2	12	30.5	29	73.5	46	117
1 1/2	38	3.8	13	33	30	76	47	119.5
1 3/4	45	4.5	14	35.5	31	79	48	122
2	50	5	15	38	32	81.5	49	124.5
2 1/2	65	6.5	16	40.5	33	84	50	127
3	75	7.5	17	43	34	86.5		
3 1/2	90	9	18	46	35	89		
4	100	10	19	48.5	36	91.5		
4 1/2	115	11.5	20	51	37	94		

KNITTING NEEDLES CONVERSION CHART

Canada/U.S.	0	1	2	3	4	5	6	7	8	9	10	10½	11	13	15
Metric (mm)	2	2¼	2¾	3¼	3½	3¾	4	4½	5	5½	6	6½	8	9	10

CROCHET HOOKS CONVERSION CHART

Canada/U.S.	1/B	2/C	3/D	4/E	5/F	6/G	8/H	9/I	10/J	10½/K	N
Metric (mm)	2.25	2.75	3.25	3.5	3.75	4.25	5	5.5	6	6.5	9.0

Annie's® *The Go-To Book for Irish Crochet Motifs* is published by Annie's, 306 East Parr Road, Berne, IN 46711. Printed in USA. Copyright © 2013, 2017 Annie's. All rights reserved. This publication may not be reproduced in part or in whole without written permission from the publisher.

RETAIL STORES: If you would like to carry this pattern book or any other Annie's publication, visit AnniesWSL.com.

Every effort has been made to ensure that the instructions in this pattern book are complete and accurate. We cannot, however, take responsibility for human error, typographical mistakes or variations in individual work. Please visit AnniesCustomerService.com to check for pattern updates.

ISBN: 978-1-59635-923-9   Library of Congress Control Number: 2015959443   10 11 12 13 14 15